At Issue

Are Books Becoming Extinct?

Other Books in the At Issue Series:

At Issue

Are Books Becoming Extinct?

David Haugen and Susan Musser, Book Editors

GREENHAVEN PRESS
A part of Gale, Cengage Learning

GALE
CENGAGE Learning·

Detroit • New York • San Francisco • New Haven, Conn • Waterville, Maine • London

Elizabeth Des Chenes, *Managing Editor*

For more information, contact:
Greenhaven Press
27500 Drake Rd.
Farmington Hills, MI 48331-3535
Or you can visit our Internet site at gale.cengage.com

For product information and technology assistance, contact us at

Gale Customer Support, 1-800-877-4253
For permission to use material from this text or product, submit all requests online at www.cengage.com/permissions.

Further permissions questions can be e-mailed to permissionrequest@cengage.com.

Articles in Greenhaven Press anthologies are often edited for length to meet page requirements. In addition, original titles of these works are changed to clearly present the main thesis and to explicitly indicate the author's opinion. Every effort is made to ensure that Greenhaven Press accurately reflects the original intent of the authors. Every effort has been made to trace the owners of copyrighted material.

Cover photograph reproduced with perission of Brand X Pictures.

LIBRARY OF CONGRESS CATALOGING-IN-PUBLICATION DATA

Are books becoming extinct? / David Haugen and Susan Musser, book editors.
p. cm. -- (At issue) Summary: 1. Digital Printing; 2. Ebooks; 3. Libraries and Ebooks; 4. Electronic Readers Are More Environmentally Friendly Than Print Books; 5. Books Are an Expendable Format, but Long-Form Writing Must Continue; 6. Books Still Matter in a Digital Age and Will Survive -- Provided by publisher.
Includes bibliographical references and index.
ISBN 978-0-7377-5546-6 -- ISBN 978-0-7377-5547-3 (pbk.)
1. Electronic publishing--Juvenile literature. 2. Electronic books--Juvenile literature. 3. Book industries and trade--Technological innovations--Juvenile literature. 4. Publishers and publishing--Forecasting--Juvenile literature. 5. Books--Forecasting--Juvenile literature. 6. Books and reading--Forecasting--Juvenile literature. I. Haugen, David M., 1969- II. Musser, Susan.
Z286.E43A74 2012
070.5'73--dc23
2011034909

Printed in the United States of America
2 3 4 5 6   16 15 14 13 12

Contents

Introduction

Although writing has been around for at least six thousand years, books are a more recent phenomenon. The form that is most recognized today, the bound book of paper pages, dates to the late Roman Empire (sometime between AD 100 and 300), and is commonly known as the codex (plural *codices*). During this period, the codex came to replace the papyrus scroll as the most prevalent form of written communication. While early codices might have been devoted to anything from tax records to poetry, it was the scholarly and religious texts of early Christianity that used the form most frequently and pioneered the way for its gradual acceptance. Christian monks saved and squirreled away many important codices when barbarian hordes swept over Europe between AD 300 and 700. Aided by book preservation efforts in Byzantium and other centers of learning, the monasteries kept alive the words of Aristotle, Hippocrates, Homer, and other luminaries of classical antiquity. The selection was important for Western culture, for these texts, resurrected in the twelfth century, became the core of academic learning, and books were the well-springs of much enlightened thought.

It is debatable whether the efforts of monks and scribes in what is often referred to as the Dark Ages (the period between AD 500 and 1000) saved scholarship from extinction in Europe, but the collections of hand-copied texts that existed did not circulate widely even by the twelfth century. Academies and noble houses kept libraries for scholars, and the majority of individuals had no access to the ideas secreted therein. In a 2010 article on academic library design for the *Library Philosophy and Practice* e-journal, Professor William T. Caniano writes, "The original libraries of the ancient world stored what was then the world of knowledge and rationed it out to suitable scholars. The libraries of the Middle Ages and Renaissance were little changed as in either case this knowledge was maintained for the privileged few." It was not until the invention of the printing press in the 1400s that formerly cloistered ideas were disseminated through mass communication. These ancient revelations were immediately joined by new scholarship that impacted science, religion, politics, and daily living. Literacy rates rose, and education, though still a privilege of the few who could afford it, touched the lives of more and more people.

Since the advent of movable type and the dissemination of printed matter, books have remained symbols of wisdom and learning. Parents are encouraged to read to their children to stimulate mental growth. Textbooks are the traditional way of passing on knowledge in academic settings. And great literature confronts readers with philosophic and moral questions about what it means to be human. As book critic David L. Ulin writes in his work *The Lost Art of Reading: Why Books Matter in a Distracted Time*, "We possess the books we read, animating the waiting stillness of their language, but they possess us also, filling us with thoughts and observations, asking us to make them part of ourselves." As commonplace as the argument may seem, individuals have their own thoughts expanded, their own hypotheses tested, and their own tastes shaped by the materials they read.

In the digital age, many commentators worry that the practice of reading is becoming, as Ulin claims, "a lost art." In 2007, the National Endowment for the Arts (NEA) released a study of America's reading habits titled *To Read or Not to Read: A Question of National Consequence*. In it, the NEA reported that average Americans between the ages of fifteen and twenty-four spent two hours a day watching television but only seven minutes reading. The survey built off of a 2004 NEA report that showed that literary reading habits had declined in America and that less than half of US adults had read a literary work in 2002, and only 56.6 percent of adults had read a book of any kind in that year. Dana Gioia, the chairman of the NEA, could not explain the decrease, but he attested that book reading "requires a degree of active attention and engagement" that stands in stark contrast to the "shorter attention spans and accelerated gratification" fostered by channel and web surfing through the glut of media available in the twenty-first century. For critics like Gioia, the concern is not that people will lose the ability to read and write but that the knowledge contained in book-length texts will no longer entice a readership raised to cull snippets of information from Internet searches. Physical, hardbound books may disappear as electronic readers and web documents gain a greater fan base, but the larger worry is that long-form writing may die out if people no longer commit the time and effort required to consume these texts.

Of course, there are observers who do fret over the possibility that physical books could become the dinosaurs of the digital age. Much of their concern stems from a nostalgic view of what books have meant to pre-Internet culture. It is difficult for many readers to give up the comfort, feel, and even smell of bound books—possessing the object equates to possessing the knowledge (potential or actualized) within. For some, the fact that electronic books are virtual texts suggests that they are impermanent and carry the same significance as any other scrap of web writing that has no physical existence. In a September 4, 2009, article for the *Boston Globe*, writer David Abel noted that this paradigm change is being felt keenly in contemporary libraries. He reports on the decision of Cushing Academy, a Massachusetts prep school, to do away with the physical books in its library in order to replace the stacks with electronic collections on e-readers and computer terminals. Abel quotes Cushing's headmaster, James Tracy, as stating, "When I look at books, I see an outdated technology, like scrolls before books. . . . We're not discouraging students from reading. We see this as a natural way to shape emerging trends and optimize technology." Cushing donated all but a few of its texts to local libraries and institutions. As of this writing, Cushing is the only US academic institution to enact such a policy.

The authors represented in *At Issue: Are Books Becoming Extinct?* address this titular question from many perspectives. Like Abel, some report on the fear that physical books are giving way to virtual texts. Others follow Gioia's argument and contend that a declining reading rate in America bespeaks a loss of appreciation and understanding of long-form writing. Some of the viewpoints within this diverse collection, however, maintain that despite such concerns, books will remain an integral part of global culture and a permanent path toward enlightenment. As *Library Journal*'s editor in chief, John Berry, once wrote, "The foundation for our new 'information society' is in the print traditions." His comment appeared in an article from June 1, 1982, the same year the concept of a world-wide network of fully interconnected TCP/IP networks called the Internet was introduced. Perhaps only now, with the advent of online texts and e-readers, can observers judge whether Berry's quote is a testimony to the durability of print traditions or the herald of a change from one mode of thinking and writing to another.

1

Digital Printing Will Destroy Book Publishing

Evan Schnittman

The former vice president of global corporate and business development at Oxford University Press, Evan Schnittman is currently managing director of group sales and marketing at Bloomsbury Publishing.

Trade book publishers traditionally rely on presale orders from retailers to generate income to cover expenses related to printing and author advances. Digital printing, however, offers no presale income. The revenue from electronic books is derived directly from consumer purchase. Although the income from direct sales to consumers may be significant for a popular title, it may take a long time to recoup costs, leaving publishers without short-term revenue to fund future projects. For this reason, e-books must remain a secondary market or risk destroying the existing publishing industry.

This piece is about consumer or "trade" publishing as we call it in the industry. To begin, let's review how a book becomes a book. A writer gets an agent who peddles a manuscript to an editor who buys the book. The publisher then pays an advance against the future royalties. (N.B., trade books' advances are often, if not nearly always, greater than the actual royalties earned.) The publisher edits, designs, produces, prints, binds, warehouses, and finally, distributes the book to

Evan Schnittman, "Why Ebooks Must Fail," *Black Plastic Glasses* (blog), March 30, 2009. http://blackplasticglasses.com.

resellers (retailers and wholesalers). Concurrently the publisher is out pre-selling in an attempt to get as many units shipped to resellers as possible.

Of all the work cited above, there are two, large-scale, out of pocket investments made by the publisher to create a trade book, the advance and the manufacturing. Advances should be viewed as controllable expenses, but in the competitive world we live in (well, used to anyway), publishers outbid each other on a regular basis to get the rights to a title. Think of it as sports fans think of free agency (in the US) or transfer fees (in Europe)—everyone thinks they are outrageously high but short of colluding, there seems to be no way to control them.

Trade books are pre-sold in far, far larger quantities than they will actually sell in a given period of time.

As to the manufacturing costs, most publishers have spent the last decade focused on systematically driving down costs in manufacturing. However, no matter how much efficiency is achieved, there is only so much that can be driven out of any process that requires skilled people and non-renewable materials. The impact of advances and manufacturing is frontloaded in the economics of book publishing. In other words, before a single dollar is earned, these costs hit the publisher. This has been the way publishing has worked for more than 100 years.

The Cycle of Advances and Returns

So how do publishers manage this difficult economic situation? We work extra hard to frontload sales by focusing marketing efforts on front list titles (Front list means this year's new titles, as opposed to backlist which means everything publisher prior to this year). Big advances (in this sense meaning lots of orders in advance of the shipping date) drive up the number of copies shipped, which is when publishers "count" the income for a book—when it is shipped from the warehouse. However, savvy readers will notice a chink in the armor—books shipped do not mean books sold.

Trade books are pre-sold in far, far larger quantities than they will actually sell in a given period of time. In fact, the bigger the title, the greater the ratio of advance to sold units. The more copies advanced, the more it will sell—but the efficiency of sales falls as the number of advance copies increases. It's a bedeviling issue for publishers as we generally sell front list to resellers on a returnable basis.

Ebooks don't have a huge returns problem, but it also means they cannot generate short-term cash flow like print books do.

Trade publishing economics is predicated on the ability of retailers to mitigate their risk and return unsold inventory for full credit. (N.B., not all retailers are designed this way—but the majority of bricks and mortar retailers in particular, are . . . especially the big box stores such as Costco who take huge positions on a relative handful of titles). So the publishers are in a funny position. To get top authors, they bid against each other and drive publishing costs through the roof. To recoup this investment, they have to pre-sell very hard and get too much inventory out onto the market, in order to bring in the cash to cover the investment. Then after some time, the unsold inventory comes back for credit, which forces us to publish more books in order to sustain our position! The cycle is never-ending and sounds all too similar to certain less than legit investment portfolios featured in recent headlines. So what does all of this have to do with ebooks?

E-books Follow Different Market Models

Well, for starters, ebooks don't follow these rules. Ebooks are effectively sold on a consignment basis—meaning the money for the sale is distributed after the sale is made, not up front.

Stores don't buy inventory, they put the file in a database and distribute copies as they are sold. This means that ebooks don't have a huge returns problem, but it also means they cannot generate short-term cash flow like print books do.

Furthermore, when you look at the pricing models that trade ebooks have engendered in the market, you see that publishers have allowed pricing to be controlled by forces that are looking to control over an emerging market rather than those who need to fund the content creation. Ebooks (at best) are selling for less than 50% of the hardcover price—often at 35–40%.

On the other hand, ebooks don't carry the same costs of print books. There are clearly no manufacturing or printing costs. However, publishers still have to buy the rights to a book no matter if that is an ebook or a print book—paying advances against royalties. There is still the need to edit, design and produce the content. In fact, many think that there are greater development costs for ebooks as electronic media opens the work to connections to the world of the web and an incredible amount of related and enhancing content—all of which needs to be managed and edited.

Ebooks, if successful, will sink the trade publishing industry.

Ebooks will still have to be sold and marketed, just in different ways as there will be far less reliance on an upfront advance buy-in, but far more reliance on ongoing marketing through the use of content and metadata—as well as user-generated content and promotion tools to get the book marketed. These are completely new expenses for publishers who traditionally think of marketing as publicity and display advertising for new books, not ongoing support and marketing for long-term sales.

Finally, the content and its metadata all need to be warehoused electronically which requires investment in technology and staff to manage the technology—be they in-house or a third party entity. Clearly ebooks aren't free—they are perhaps as expensive or in some cases more expensive than print—yet they do not create large, short-term cash flow to cover their costs. Ebooks, if successful, will sink the trade publishing industry.

E-books Cannot Stand Alone

And therein lies the dilemma . . . how does the publishing industry fund the creation, editing, design, production, marketing, e-warehousing, and sales of ebooks, if the income isn't there? How do ebooks cover the huge advances needed to buy books if we cannot generate the cash, especially at their extremely low, discounted prices, cover the advances that an entire industry has come to require? The answer is that ebooks, alone, cannot.

What this means is that unless a very different model evolves, ebooks can never become the dominant version of content sold by book publishers. It means that ebooks will always be priced to sell, but sold as an afterthought, not as the primary version of a work. It means that the need for blended e plus p [electronic plus print] models will evolve, in order to take advantage of all the great qualities of ebooks, while providing the financial support and structure that print offers. It means that consumer ebooks, as a stand-alone version of an intellectual property, must fail.

2

Digital Printing Will Save Book Publishing

Nic Boshart

Nic Boshart is the digital services manager at the Association of Canadian Publishers. He also serves as coordinating editor of Invisible Publishing, a company that helps independent writers create marketable books.

Digital printing will not destroy traditional publishing, though it may help clean up some of its wasteful practices. Print publishing uses a lot of energy and materials in the manufacture and transport of physical books. E-books, on the other hand, are comparatively better for the environment and can reduce many of a publisher's costs. Beyond considerations of waste, e-books will offer alternatives to publishers who wish to expand certain markets, giving them new sources of revenue and enticing them to reduce costs to customers. Electronic printing will also put pressure on those publishers who continue printing physical books to make better-quality, more-attractive products. In short, customers and publishers will win as e-book publishing continues to grow.

The headlines scream apocalypse, but the truth is that wasteful practices have been devaluing book publishing for decades. For savvy publishers, the digital revolution delivering Kindles, iPads, Kobos and other new gadgets is actually leading to a more sustainable future—economically *and* ecologically.

Nic Boshart, "Brave New Book World: Digital Printing and Electronic Readers Will Save Publishing, Not Kill It," *Alternatives Journal*, vol. 37, no. 3, 2011, pp. 22–23. Copyright © 2011 by Alternatives, Inc. All rights reserved. Reproduced by permission from the author and *Alternatives Journal*, www.alternativesjournal.ca.

Books today travel a long way. Many begin life in China, are shipped across oceans to warehouses, are loaded onto trucks and then delivered to stores. Retailers return those that they don't sell to the publisher (for a full refund) to be slowly resold or, as a last resort, to be pulped. On average, returns constitute 30 to 40 per cent of the print run. It's even worse for a bestseller that bombs, which can result in 80 per cent of the print run being returned unsold. Thanks to new technologies, though, this picture is quickly changing, and both publishers and bookstores stand to benefit.

With print-on-demand (POD) technology, a book is made only after it is sold. That means less or no physical stock-on-hand, lower warehouse costs and fewer returns.

More Environmentally Friendly

The e-book is the biggest new factor. Last December [2010] US chain Barnes and Noble reported that its online e-book sales outstripped sales of hard copy books for the first time. Critics rightly point out that e-readers, which contain heavy metals and consume multiple resources during production, are a long way from sustainable. The devices are also shipped around the world. However, proponents say the carbon footprint can be offset if enough e-books are purchased instead of physical books. (Market research firm Cleantech Group says a Kindle has a carbon footprint equivalent to that of 22½ books, but that figure is difficult to verify as Amazon declined to provide information about its manufacturing process.) Still, as electronics manufacturing improves, life-cycle impacts will likely improve too.

There is room to lighten paper's foot print as well. With print-on-demand (POD) technology, a book is made only after it is sold. That means less or no physical stock-on-hand, lower warehouse costs and fewer returns. One device, the Espresso Book Machine, can print, cut and bind a book in less than five minutes at about a penny a page. While that is considerably more expensive than large-run printing, these units are turning up at university bookstores and we will eventually see a POD-only bookstore.

Faced with the thrifty allure of e-books, . . . publishers will have to create more beautiful hard-copy editions to justify the purchase of an object.

Hardcovers Will Remain for Collectors

Industry insiders expect paperbacks to be the first to disappear from physical existence since they tend to be mass marketed to people more interested in reading than in physical books. The average mystery and romance reader consumes two or more books a week. For these readers, access and price—fields in which e-books shine—are hefty considerations. Indeed, the romance community has formed one of the first digital publishing imprints, Carina Press.

The last bastion of tradition is the books-as-objects aficionados. Like vinyl LPs, certain books will always be collectors items. Faced with the thrifty allure of e-books, though, publishers will have to create more beautiful hard-copy editions to justify the purchase of an object. Environmentally friendly paper and ink, and local production will matter.

The Internet, meanwhile, helps level the field for authors and independent publishers everywhere, enabling them to reach an international readership. There will still be blockbuster books, but there will also be a more equitable distribution of sales among other titles. Using social media, authors can build and maintain a global audience.

Reinvigorating All Forms of Publishing

While digital delivery transformed music and news consumption, it won't change how we read books. When music went digital, you no longer had to buy an entire album for one song. The Internet delivered news as it happened, not only at 6 and 11 o'clock. But reading a digital book is no faster than reading a physical one; chapters, unlike songs, don't often stand alone; and immediacy isn't much of an issue for books, especially fiction.

The Internet, meanwhile, helps level the field for authors and independent publishers everywhere, enabling them to reach an international readership.

The change has been societal. Early e-book readers like the Apple Newton—introduced in 1993 and dumped by 1998—failed because we had not yet become addicted to having content at our finger tips. With the advent of smartphones, our new buying habits have conditioned us to live digitally. We expect the content we want, when we want it.

Publishers will respond. Exciting authors will be easier to discover. Digital titles will find physical form at the corner POD kiosk. And since book lovers will still want nice objects, there will be a new age of book craftsmanship. Paper waste and print runs are dying, but long live the book!

3

Digital Printing Will Destroy Traditional Supply and Retail Book Markets

Richard Nash

Richard Nash was formerly the publisher of Soft Skull Press. He is currently a publishing industry consultant and is working on a niche social publishing community start-up called Cursor.

By 2020, the publishing landscape will unavoidably change. Digital publishing will bring more written works to the hands of readers, and brick-and-mortar stores and retail venues will falter. Publishers who are failing to plan for the dominance of electronic publishing will fade, while many bookstores and outlets will become obsolete. Those publishing houses that survive or begin operating in the modern, Internet age will face questions not about how to increase sales of written works but how to predict and satisfy audience demand. Happily, that demand will remain strong as the Internet obviates old business models and alters how most people will acquire and experience printed texts.

In the lead up to the most recent New Year (2010), a flurry of op-ed style activity occurred around predicting the developments of the year and I was asked to offer up a few. I found the prospect, frankly, boring. More stimulating, I thought, would be to contemplate publishing developments 10 years out.

Why is a 10 year prediction easier than a 1 year prediction? Surely the less far into the future one must speculate, the

Richard Nash, "Publishing 2020," *Publishing Research Quarterly*, vol. 26, April 13, 2010, pp. 114–118.

less likely one could be wrong? Ordinarily yes, as with, say, the climate, the economy, the next gadget. But with trade publishing, the next year is effectively in the hands of the CEO's of the corporate publishers and the retailers of print and digital books.

In that respect, I am reminded of one of the key fictional disciplines in [science fiction author Isaac] Asimov's *Foundation* trilogy, psychohistory. It could never predict the actions of an individual, but by applying statistical analysis to a sociology/history hybrid, it could predict long-term trends in human social development (Paul Krugman recently admitted the reason he became an economist was that economics was as close as he could get to psychohistory.)

While psychohistory is a fictional "science," applying some history, sociology and economics to publishing (and publishing prognoses) might in fact be a good idea. Especially because while it's a commonplace that smaller independent publishers might be ill-versed in the ways of markets and capitalism, we have failed to notice how astonishingly ignorant corporate publishing is.

Corporate publishing management's goal is clearly to minimize disruption in the short-term and focus on maximizing personal power through acquisitions (of big-ticket books, of companies).

Economically Irrational

It is axiomatic in economics that auctions almost always result in the "winner" overpaying, a phenomenon called "Winner's Curse," though one could easily say, the winner of the auction is in fact the loser. The worst offenders in this regard are corporate publishers, not the independents; it is the corporates who are the most economically irrational.

Why? Well, top management in book publishing corporations, indeed in any corporation, are largely interested in personal survival. As most recently elaborated in [a 2009 book by Jonathan A. Knee, Bruce C. Greenwald, and Ava Seave] *The Curse of the Mogul,* most media companies are run by managers who operate in their own interests, not on behalf of shareholders. (And who could blame them—it is the [failed] corporate governance system, not self-abnegation, that is supposed to align their interests with the shareholders.) The recent financial meltdown suggests that the finance industry is equally beset.

Unless one CEO arises who . . . lays off about 50% of the workforce and utterly reconstitutes the company . . . all the corporate publishers will be gone in 10 years.

Corporate publishing management's goal is clearly to minimize disruption in the short-term and focus on maximizing personal power through acquisitions (of bigticket books, of companies), a publishing instance of what is called in more general business circles, IBGYBG ("I'll be gone, you'll be gone," we'll pocket the bonuses and move on.) All the current debates about pricing, discounts, publishing windows, and so forth have little to do with the future of publishing, and everything to do with keeping senior management in place for as long as possible. This is understandable—if you had to choose between saving your job, and saving your industry, which would you pick?

It has been remarkable to see how many people put the blame on profit-seeking when explaining what is wrong in US trade publishing when in fact most top management activity—the "Winner's Curse" above, buying other publishing businesses, maintaining an enormous real estate footprint in midtown Manhattan, in fact everything other than laying off underlings—has had the effect of hurting profit margins. The notion that profit-seeking is destroying publishing is a fantasy, really, it is a lack of entrepreneurial capitalism that is destroying publishing, for decades now, obscured only by their access to working capital.

While I am not arguing that capitalism is the best form of social organization, especially as it pertains to culture-making, it is very clear that the crony capitalism practiced in the Western media industries is far worse than entrepreneurial late modern capitalism. Entrepreneurial capitalism does not need saving, because when it fails, it fails quickly, and when it succeeds others learn from it. It telegraphs where society can best allocate resources. The structure of the publishing industry right now not only misallocates resources, it is *incapable* of learning.

So, unless one CEO arises who, I am appalled to see myself write, lays off about 50% of the workforce and utterly reconstitutes the company (as IBM did 1990–1995) all the forgoing leads to one significant prediction—that *all* the corporate publishers will be gone in 10 years. Maybe one or two companies might semi-resemble a corporate publisher of now, though they will publish perhaps 100 books a year, all blockbusters or would-be blockbusters, and those companies will be continually on the edge of going out of business.

The bricks-and-mortar chains will be gone, since their strength, selection, will be ever less relevant.

The Marketplace Will Change

The companies that will be at the center of the reading-writing economy in 2020, therefore, will be companies that likely do not exist now, with the probable exception of Amazon who will endure a Microsoft-like diminution of market power, given that their competitive advantage has always been more in print than digital. The bricks-and-mortar chains will be gone, since their strength, selection, will be ever less relevant, and the strength of the boutique retailer, taste, is unavailable to them. So Borders, B&N, BAM will go the way of retailers like Circuit City, Tower Records, Virgin Megastore and Sharper Image and a couple hundred bricks-and-mortar venues will be central to book culture, functioning like Other Music, the Apple Store, Giant Robot, while certain books will continue to penetrate precisely those kinds of retailers I just compared the successful bookstores to.

The price of raw digital content will have been zero for quite a while, just as it is now for music, news, TV, and film, though plenty of effective market mechanisms will arise to pay both authors—the majority of whom will generate more revenue in 2020 than they did in 2010, though there will no longer be the fantasy of hitting the big advance lottery—and to pay intermediaries who help connect authors to readers in what is called a "multi-sided marketplace."

What will this marketplace look like? I'm reminded of the comments of Gavin Potter in a *Wired* magazine piece by mathematician and novelist Jordan Ellenberg—"The 20th century was about sorting out supply," Potter said. "The 21st is going to be about sorting out demand." The article explored the response to the offering by Netflix, a DVD rental company of a prize of one million dollars to the person(s) who could improve their movie-recommending algorithm by 10%. "The Netflix challenge," wrote Ellenberg, is just one example of a kind of problem called *data mining*—trying to make useful sense out of a gigantic dataset, typically rather noisy, completely unintelligible to the naked eye, and, despite its size, often painfully incomplete. Data mining is what Google does when it transforms the vast and ever-changing array of links on the Web into one number, PageRank, which it uses to figure out which page comes up first in your search. It's what intelligence agencies do—or at least what we surmise they do—when they search for red-flag patterns in a heterogeneous stew of visa applications, phone calls, and flight and hotel reservations. Amazon does precisely this when it makes recommendations based on your purchasing patterns, using what's called kNN, "k-nearest-neighbor algorithm," although Netflix's efforts go deeper, adding dimensions along which viewers—hi-middle-lo-brow—vary, and along which films vary—horror, romcom, sci-fi, and so forth.

What Potter is hinting at, is that the area on which he is focusing, what could be called match-making movies with viewers, supply with demand, is a relatively new problem. And if you look at the recent history of trade publishing you will see he is in fact correct. Pretty much every technological advance in publishing has centered around solving supply. From the deployment of microfiche by Ingram in the early 1970s to assist booksellers in ascertaining what Ingram's inventory levels were on given titles, to the invention of PageMaker, Quark, and Photoshop, to the invention of digital printing, invention and innovation has had the effect of permitting an increase in the number of titles that can be either created or managed by the supply chain.

The Need for Demand-Side Innovations

Indeed, most social and political developments have had the same effect—the expansion of tertiary education, the GI Bill, diminutions in more explicit forms of racism, sexism, and anti-immigrant bigotry all contributed to a dramatic increase in the number of people with the social, intellectual, cultural and financial capital to create long-form narratives.

Relatively little innovation has occurred on the demand side, a process ably documented by Ted Striphas in *The Late Age of Print*, a superb book I reviewed for *The Critical Flame* [in 2009] and which I won't rehearse here except to note the particularly colorful example of ineffective demand-side innovation—a PR [public relations] firm hired to persuade architects and interior designers to install more bookshelves in apartments and houses so as to increase demand for books to fill them.

To explore further what the implications of this for the "publishing" business models of 2020, I would like to refer to a second article on the same topic of the Netflix prize, published 8 months after the initial *Wired* article, in *The New York Times Magazine*. The article in part examined what movies were the grit in the gears, the movies that had slowed the process of getting to ten percent for all the prize entrants what those movies have in common is that they are idiosyncratic voice and character-driven artworks, replete with ironic humor—*I Heart Huckabees, Napoleon Dynamite, Lost in Translation, The Life Aquatic With Steve Zissou,* and *Sideways.* Much like most contemporary Western literary fiction. Put bluntly: novels break algorithms.

Agents, publishers, retailers, media were effectively the four set of intermediaries between writer and reader in varying measures over the past 150 years—so what replaces them?

What this entails are human intermediaries, therefore. When you stop to consider that at the present juncture, we are producing a half million new titles a year distributed amongst, say, thirty million readers, were confronted with sample sizes of overlapping readership for the vast majority of texts that are so miniscule, no mathematician could possibly build a model that could predict likes and dislikes. (Netflix, by contrast, has a dataset comprising "only" 17,770 Netflix movies, a tiny fraction of the book output.)

My own predictions, therefore, begin to break down here. For if we agree that there will be intermediaries, but also agree there will be no supply chain, how will intermediaries organize themselves? Agents, publishers, retailers, media were effectively the four set of intermediaries between writer and reader in varying measures over the past 150 years—so what replaces them? Here I cannot answer except to note that the price of digital content is zero, and yet even presently the word "book" appears on more than one percent of all tweets. This suggests that book reading drives social conversation—the future intermediaries are going to be interfacing with dimension.

Any time technology has increased the number of people who can create, disseminate, and consume knowledge, the existing gatekeepers have decried it as signaling the end of civilization.

Reading Culture will Live On

Notwithstanding the limitations on my predictions on how the shape of intermediating structures will look in 2020, I'm quite confident that the endless media hoo-haa about the death of the book, and the death of reading will slowly fade away, going the way of the articles of last century about TV destroying radio and film and books. (The death of the eBook, much like the death of the CD and the coming demise of the mp3, will provoke relatively few histrionics—as connectivity becomes ever more pervasive through 4G, WiMax etc., all text will be in the cloud, and the need for files vanishes.) It becomes clear that roughly the same percentage of the population continues to read immersive text-only long form narrative and that the proliferation of multimodal forms in art, entertainment and education are precisely that, the creation of something new, and not the destruction of books, or painting. Many writers will choose to write in multimodal forms, just as many novelists currently write screenplays, and a few write videogames. The absence of audio, video and branching narratives within text-only long form narrative will be recognized for what it has always been, a feature, not a bug.

However, articles on the death of culture will continue. Any time technology has increased the number of people who can create, disseminate, and consume knowledge, the existing gatekeepers have decried it as signaling the end of civilization. This phenomenon goes as far back as we can keep track of this impulse, to Socrates bemoaning the use of the book to avoid memorization and continues throughout history, through [printing press inventor Johannes] Gutenberg and the loss of control over translations of the Bible, through the nineteenth century and the panic over fiction destroying the minds and morals of young women, through the moral panic of the 1950s over comics and the pulp novel, to the present reactionary idiocies of [Sven] Birkerts [who believes e-books may reduce the humanity of authors to a mere collection of data] and [Mark] Helprin [who wants to extend copyright laws so that writers and their families retain publishing rights longer]. Given that access to culture-making is going to continue to explode, especially in the developing world, we can expect ever more of this, and culture-centric screeds against technology will develop an ever more racist/xenophobic quality (not all, just more) as billions more Africans, Indians and Asians enter the middle-class and start reading and writing narrative, just as Westerners did in the past century.

Too much to possibly happen in a decade? Remember: two and a half decades from now, the iPhone's computing power will fit inside a blood cell.

4

E-books Will Replace Disposable Bound Books

Craig Mod

Craig Mod is a writer, designer, and publisher whose articles on the future of books have appeared in the New Scientist *and the* New York Times. *He is the coauthor of* Art Space Tokyo *and the cofounder of the storytelling project Hitotoki, an online repository of life experiences and travel narratives from participants around the world.*

Digital publishing will not do away with all print publishing, but it will thankfully eliminate disposable books, such as pocketbooks, pulp fiction, and any other mass-market texts that do not require a printed format. This will force publishers to print only those works that utilize page layout as an inherent means of conveying content. However, new digital devices, such as the Apple iPad, are enabling bookmakers to electronically distribute some of these works that employ visually interesting content, so the number of these texts that go digital may increase. Furthermore, the new electronic tablet technology will allow book designers to create new works that specifically take advantage of this new medium, opening more opportunities for clever, artistic, content-driven publications.

As the publishing industry wobbles and Kindle sales jump, book romanticists cry themselves to sleep. But really, what are we shedding tears over?

We're losing the throwaway paperback.

The airport paperback.

The beachside paperback.

We're losing the dregs of the publishing world: *disposable books*. The book printed without consideration of form or sustainability or longevity. The book produced to be consumed once and then tossed. The book you bin when you're moving and you need to clean out the closet.

These are the first books to go. And I say it again, *good riddance*.

The Benefits of Digital Formats

Once we dump this weight we can prune our increasingly obsolete network of distribution. As physicality disappears, so too does the need to fly dead trees around the world.

You already know the potential gains: edgier, riskier books in digital form, born from a lower barrier-to-entry to publish. New modes of storytelling. Less environmental impact. A rise in importance of editors. And, yes—paradoxically—a marked increase in the quality of things that *do* get printed.

With the iPad we finally have a platform for consuming rich-content in digital form.

From 2003–2009 I spent six years trying to make beautiful printed books. Six years. Focused on printed books. In the 00s.

And I loved it. I loved the process. The finality of the end product. I loved the sexy-as-hell tactility of those little ink and paper bricks. But I can tell you this: the excitement I feel about the iPad as a content creator, designer and publisher—and the potential it brings must be acknowledged. Acknowledged bluntly and with perspective.

With the iPad we finally have a platform for consuming rich-content in digital form. What does that mean? To understand just why the iPad is so exciting we need to think about how we got here.

I want to look at where printed books stand in respect to digital publishing, why we historically haven't read long-form text on screens and how the iPad is wedging itself in the middle of everything. In doing so I think we can find the line in the sand to define when content should be printed or digitized.

This is a conversation for books-makers, web-heads, content-creators, authors and designers. For people who love beautifully made things. And for the storytellers who are willing to take risks and want to consider the most appropriate shape and media for their yarns.

The true value of an object lies in what it says, not its mere existence.

Focusing on Forms Worth Printing

For too long, the act of printing something in and of itself has been placed on too high a pedestal. The true value of an object lies in what it says, not its mere existence. And in the case of a book, that value is intrinsically connected with content.

Let's divide content into two broad groups.

- Content without well-defined form (Formless Content)

- Content with well-defined form (Definite Content)

Formless Content can be reflowed into different formats and not lose any intrinsic meaning. It's content divorced from layout. Most novels and works of non-fiction are Formless.

When Danielle Steele sits at her computer, she doesn't think much about how the text will look printed. She thinks about the story as a waterfall of text, as something that can be poured into any container. *(Actually, she probably just thinks awkward and sexy things, but awkward and sexy things without regard for final form.)*

Content with form—Definite Content—is almost totally the opposite of Formless Content. Most texts composed with images, charts, graphs or poetry fall under this umbrella. It may be reflowable, but depending on how it's reflowed, inherent *meaning and quality* of the text may shift.

You can sure as hell bet that author Mark Z. Danielewski is well aware of the final form of his next novel. His content is so Definite it's actually impossible to digitize and retain all of the original meaning. *Only Revolutions*, a book loathed by many, forces readers to flip between the stories of two characters. The start of each printed at opposite ends of the book.

A designer may, of course, working in concert with the author, imbue Formless Content with additional meaning in layout. The final combination of design and text becoming Definite Content.

For an extreme and ubiquitous contemporary example of Definite Content, see [Edward R.] Tufte. Love him or hate him, you have to admit he's a rare combination of author and designer, completely obsessed with final form, meaning and perfection in layout.

Formless Content doesn't see the page or its boundaries. Whereas Definite Content is not only aware of the page, but embraces it.

In the context of the book as an object, the key difference between Formless and Definite Content is the interaction between the content and the page. Formless Content doesn't *see* the page or its boundaries. Whereas Definite Content is not only aware of the page, but *embraces* it. It edits, shifts and resizes itself to fit the page. In a sense, Definite Content approaches the page as a canvas—something with dimensions and limitations—and leverages these attributes to both elevate the object and the content to a more complete whole.

Put very simply, Formless Content is unaware of the container. Definite Content embraces the container as a canvas. Formless content is usually only text. Definite content usually has some visual elements along with text.

Digital Formats for Formless Content

Much of what we consume happens to be Formless. The bulk of printed matter—novels and non-fiction—is Formless.

In the last two years, devices excelling at displaying Formless Content have multiplied—the Amazon Kindle being most obvious. Less obvious are devices like the iPhone, whose extremely high resolution screen, despite being small, makes longer texts much more comfortable to read than traditional digital displays.

In other words, it's now easier and more comfortable than ever to consume Formless Content in a digital format.

Is it as *comfortable* as reading a printed book?

Maybe not. But we're getting closer.

When people lament the loss of the printed book, this—comfort—is usually what they're talking about. *My eyes tire more easily*, they say. *The batteries run out, the screen is tough to read in sunlight. It doesn't like bath tubs.*

Important to note is that these aren't complaints about the text losing *meaning*. Books don't become harder to understand, or confusing just because they're digital. It's mainly issues concerning quality. One inevitable property of the quality argument is that technology is closing the gap (through advancements in screens and batteries) and because of additional features (note taking, bookmarking, searching), will inevitably surpass the comfort level of reading on paper.

The convenience of digital text—on demand, lightweight (in file size and physicality), searchable—already far trumps that of traditional printed matter.

The formula used to be simple: stop printing Formless Content; only print well-considered Definite Content.

The iPad changes this.

The convenience of digital text—on demand, lightweight (in file size and physicality), searchable—already far trumps that of traditional printed matter.

The iPad Enables New Reading Experiences

It's no wonder we love our printed books—we physically cradle them close to our heart. Unlike computer screens, the experience of reading on a Kindle or iPhone (or iPad, one can assume) mimics this familiar maternal embrace. The text is closer to us, the orientation more comfortable. And the seemingly insignificant fact that we touch the text actually plays a very key role in furthering the intimacy of the experience.

The Kindle and iPhone are both lovely—but they only do text.

The iPad changes the experience formula. It brings the excellent text readability of the iPhone/Kindle to a larger canvas. It combines the intimacy and comfort of reading on those devices with a canvas *both* large enough and versatile enough to allow for well considered layouts.

What does this mean? Well, most obviously that a 1:1 digital adaptation of Definite Content books will now be possible. However, I don't think this is a solution we should blindly embrace. Definite Content in printed books is laid out *specifically* for that canvas, that page size. While the iPad may be similar in physical scope to those books, duplicating layouts would be a disservice to the new canvas and modes of interaction introduced by the iPad.

Take something as fundamental as pages, for example. The metaphor of flipping pages already feels *boring and forced* on the iPhone. I suspect it will feel even more so on the iPad.

The flow of content no longer has to be chunked into 'page' sized bites. One simplistic reimagining of book layout would be to place chapters on the horizontal plane with content on a fluid vertical plane.

We're going to see new forms of storytelling emerge from this [iPad] canvas.

In printed books, the two-page spread was our canvas. It's easy to think similarly about the iPad. Let's not. The canvas of the iPad must be considered in a way that acknowledges the physical boundaries of the device, while also embracing the effective limitlessness of space just beyond those edges.

We're going to see new forms of storytelling emerge from this canvas. This is an opportunity to redefine modes of conversation between reader and content. And that's one hell of an opportunity if making content is your thing.

Questions on the Future of Publishing

So: Are Printed Books Dead? Not quite.

The rules for iPad content are still ambiguous. None of us has had enough time with the device to confidently define them. I have, however, spent six years thinking about materials, form, physicality and content and to the best of my humble abilities—producing printed books.

So, for now, here's my take on the print side of things moving forward.

Ask yourself, "Is your work disposable?" For me, in asking myself this, I only see one obvious ruleset:

- Formless Content goes digital.

- Definite Content gets divided between the iPad and printing.

Of the books we do print—the books we make—they need rigor. They need to be books where the object is embraced as a canvas by designer, publisher and writer. This is the only way these books as physical objects will carry any meaning moving forward.

I propose the following to be considered whenever we think of printing a book:

- The Books We Make embrace their physicality—working in concert with the content to illuminate the narrative.

- The Books We Make are confident in form and usage of material.

- The Books We Make exploit the advantages of print.

- The Books We Make are built to last.

The result of this is:

- The Books We Make will feel whole and solid in the hands.

- The Books We Make will smell like now forgotten, far away libraries.

- The Books We Make will be something of which even our children—who have fully embraced all things digital—will understand the worth.

- The Books We Make will always remind people that the printed book can be a sculpture for thoughts and ideas.

Anything less than this will be stepped over and promptly forgotten in the digital march forward.

Goodbye disposable books.

Hello new canvases.

5

E-books Will Not Replace Bound Books

Rundy Purdy

Rundy Purdy is the author of two novels, The Stuttering Bard of York *and* Arielle's Wedding, *and a number of uncollected essays.*

Electronic books will never achieve dominance in the book publishing marketplace. They are too expensive in comparison to bound books, even though it is clear that they cost less to produce. Customers will not be fooled into spending more for books, especially in the current recession. In addition, e-book readers are also overpriced, placing them only in the hands of those well-off enough to afford such extravagance. Most readers will continue to cling to fair-priced paperbacks because they are not an expensive investment and they can be taken anywhere without fear of loss or damage.

It is all the rage now to say that ebooks are the future of publishing. There is no better way to make yourself a predictable sage then to proclaim that ebooks herald the demise of paper books, and in a decade we'll see scarcely a printed book around. Or something like that. While I have gone on the record to say that we are in the middle of a publishing revolution, I believe these popular predictions about ebooks are wrong. Ebooks *will* have a part of the publishing future, but they will not cause paper books to become nearly extinct. Ebooks will surely remain a minority player in the book publishing field.

Pros and Cons of Ebooks

I'm not the first to speak against the hype of ebooks. The typical arguments for ebooks are the litany of cheap, easy, convenient. The usual arguments against ebooks from doom-sayers are the chants of difficult, inconvenient, and aesthetically displeasing. Depending on who is making the argument, different people lay stress on different points. Jason Epstein in his 2009 O'Reilly Tools of Change for Publishing speech laid a special emphasis on the aesthetic aspect of physical books. Other people will complain about the lack of readability of digital screens, or the frustrations of handling ebooks. While there is merit to each of these complaints, none of them get to the heart of why ebooks will not take over the publishing industry.

The real reason ebooks will not conquer the publishing world is simple: The cost of reading ebooks is too high.

The real reason ebooks will not conquer the publishing world is simple: The cost of reading ebooks is too high. This cost comes in two parts: The cost of ebooks, and the cost of ebook readers.

The Cost of Ebooks

Theoretically, an ebook could cost nothing. The cost of transmitting the digital bits of ebooks is nil. This is why you can find ebooks for works in the public domain available for free all over the Internet. But if sending an ebook across the world to a thousand people costs nothing, writing an ebook takes time, and most authors want some monetary compensation for their time. And if authors are getting something, publishers want a piece of it too. The problem is that publishing companies are damaging the prospects of ebooks by their standard practice of inflating the price for ebooks.

As of this writing, (June 2010,) if you go online to Amazon or Barnes and Noble you will see most popular and recently released ebooks priced in the range of $10. For example, today at Amazon the ebook of *The Shack* by William P. Young is priced at $9.99. There are several problems with this pricing picture. The most obvious is the paperback offering of the book for $8.47 with free Super Saver Shipping. You can purchase a paperback copy for *less* than the ebook copy. "Now wait a minute," you think. "An ebook which costs nothing to print is being sold for more than a book which costs something to print?" This type of situation will not encourage the success of ebooks.

In its own offerings Amazon prices the paperback copy higher than the ebook copy of the same title—but only by a little bit (in this case 20 cents, for a price of $10.19). However, the fact that third party sellers can offer the new paperback for *significantly* less indicates that Amazon's pricing is an artifical peg, neatly kept just above the desired price peg for the ebooks.

Publishers are afraid they might ruin the market for paperback books if ebooks were made much cheaper, so the price of ebooks is inflated to just below the cost of paperbacks to make ebooks less attractive.

The more we look at this pricing structure, the worse it appears. It actually costs something to print and ship a paperback book, but how much? To continue with our example of *The Shack*, there are third party booksellers selling a new paperbook copy for as low as $5.45 (with an additional cost of $3.99 for shipping). This price tells us retailers can pick up this book for under $5.45. Since the cost of distributing ebooks is effectively nonexistent, if a paperback copy of a book can be sold for $5.45, then the ebook should be sold for *at least* that low a price. But let's not stop there. Ebooks don't require paper and ink to create. That should be an additional savings. Using POD [print on demand] I could print a book like *The Shack* for about $4.00. But it costs less to print a book in large off-set print runs, so let's say it only costs the publisher $2.00 to print *The Shack*. Since there is no similar printing cost for the ebook, the ebook copy ought to cost *no more* than $3.45. Instead, we have the ebook priced at $9.99.

The Influence of Greed and Fear

Why is there this huge price markup in ebooks? There are two basic reasons: Greed, and fear. Publishers are afraid they might ruin the market for paperback books if ebooks were made much cheaper, so the price of ebooks is inflated to just below the cost of paperbacks to make ebooks *less* attractive. This appeals to both the publishers and retailers of ebooks because it means they can make *huge* profits from ebooks. There is no cost to print or stock ebooks—all of the printing and distributing costs are turned into pure profit gravy.

This pricing structure is neither fair to the consumer, nor truly wise on the part of the publishers and retailers. If you want your product to be successful, make it as affordable as possible, and treat your customers right. Instead, what we currently have in the ebook market is a form of price fixing. Publishers and retailers can reap large profits from ebooks, but the over-pricing depresses the market for ebooks. Until publishers and retailers adjust their prices to a fair level, the market for ebooks will be severely stunted. People know a bad deal when they see it.

To conveniently read ebooks you need an ebook reader, and this will remain a prohibitive cost for most people.

The Cost of Ebook Readers

Even if publishers and retailers reform their practices and begin selling ebooks at a fair price, ebooks still will not take over the entire publishing market. The issue of cost remains—the cost of ebook readers. To conveniently read ebooks you need an ebook reader, and this will remain a prohibitive cost for most people.

At any given time in the United States, between 13% and 17% of the population is below the poverty line, and within a ten year period 40% of the population will fall below the poverty line. Over half of Americans will at some point live in poverty. I have lived in poverty, and from my own experience I can tell you that if someone is living in poverty they simply cannot afford a $200 ebook reader, not even a $150, or $100 ebook reader (much less the current price of $250+). Even those not in poverty, but with limited disposable income, will be reluctant or unwilling to invest in such a device.

For a large segment of the population, the cost of entry into ebook reading will remain unfeasible and this has a profound impact on the viability of ebooks.

Most people are going to continue buying cheap paperback books for their recreational reading.

If this were not enough, a bit of math quickly makes it apparent that for most people it makes no economic sense to use an ebook reader. Currently a Kindle costs $259, a Nook $259, and the Ipad $499. According to a poll taken by Associated Press-Ipsos in 2007, of those who read books the median number of books read was nine books per year for women, and five for men. At $10 for a paperback book (mass market paperbacks are typically a few dollars less, a trade paperback possibly a little more) it would take the median woman reader in this survey nearly *three years* of reading on her ebook reader before she would have spent as much on physical books as it cost her to purchase on her ebook reader—*and that without counting the cost of any ebook purchases!* At these prices you are spending *more* money to use ebooks, not less.

For your average reader it makes no economic sense to use ebooks. More than that, it is not practical. What are you going to do—bring a $6.00 mass market paperback to the beach, or your expensive ebook reader? Most people will take a cheap paperback. What are you going to do—use one ebook reader for everyone in the family so only one person can read one book at a time, buy an ebook reader for everyone in the family, or buy one paper copy of each book so everyone can read whichever book they want? The affluent in society can afford to buy an ebook reader for every member of the family, and chance losing or destroying their ebook reader at the beach, but most people are not affluent. Most people are going to continue buying cheap paperback books for their recreational reading.

Ebooks Will Not Rule Publishing's Future

Do ebooks have a place in the future of publishing? Yes, ebooks have a place in the future of publishing, especially to niche markets. If publishers bring the cost of ebooks down to a fair and appropriate level, the market for ebooks will expand, and if the cost of ebook readers declines, the market segment will thrive. But will ebooks rule the future of publishing? No, because it will always cost more to produce a sophisticated electronic ebook reader than it costs to produce the bundle of paper we call books. For this reason ebooks will always have a minority share in the publishing world. How successful that share becomes depends on how intelligently publishers, and authors, develop the market.

6

Libraries Need to Face the Challenges Presented by E-books

Eric Hellman

Eric Hellman is a technology developer for libraries. He was the director of OCLC Openly Informatics (which became OCLC New Jersey), a business that develops software and information networks for libraries.

Academic and public libraries will soon be faced with challenges caused by the widespread availability and dissemination of electronic books. Instead of waiting to see what happens in this new electronic culture, libraries need to be proactive, figuring out how to provide patrons with e-books and offering new services that can help patrons navigate and evaluate digital material. As electronic books and wi-fi access become more available from bookstores and coffee shops, so libraries must act quickly to promote their strengths and their special offerings in order to show that these venerable institutions will not become obsolete in the digital age.

People keep writing articles about how valuable libraries are, even with ebooks and the Internet and all. Well, duh. Of course libraries are important. What people are overlooking is that the reason libraries are having such fits dealing with a changing environment is *not* that libraries are unrecog-

Eric Hellman, "Libraries, Ebooks, and Competition," *Library Journal*, vol. 135, no. 13, August 1, 2010, pp. 22–23. Copyright © 2010 by Library Journals LLC. All rights reserved. Reproduced by permission.

nized as fountains of value, it's that libraries are *so* valuable that they attract voracious new competition with every technological advance.

The Internet Has Changed Libraries

To give you an example, 16 years ago I would go to my local public library to keep track of the latest news about companies whose stocks I owned. The financial information I got at the library was something I could take to the bank, so to speak. It would be pretty silly to do that today. All sorts of finance websites recognized that with advertising support, they could capture some of the value that used to be in libraries. Now, thanks to this competition, I get more timely, better quality financial information, in the middle of the night, from my chair. The library book I best remember reading as a teenager was Dostoyevsky's *Crime and Punishment*. I borrowed it from the county library and read it on the beach at the New Jersey shore. Today, it's likely that a teenager would get the same book from Project Gutenberg and read it on a smartphone without ever visiting a library.

The Internet has made it possible for businesses and nonprofit websites to beat out libraries and capture value.

The Internet has made it possible for businesses and nonprofit websites to beat out libraries and capture value. And vice versa. Free Internet is offered by 82 percent of public libraries in the United States; 67 percent of the libraries report that they are the only place providing that type of access to their communities. The Internet has enabled academic libraries to offer new and more comprehensive services where the need has been greatest. Today, typical students or scholars have access to a much larger swath of knowledge through their library than a pre-Internet library could have imagined offering.

Overall, the Internet has resulted in both increases and decreases in the value delivered by libraries; libraries continue to attract funding from institutions and communities, while many measures of library usage have showed steady increases.

The survival of libraries will depend on their ability to take advantage of ebook technologies to deliver new kinds of value, even as competition arises in the delivery of their traditional services.

Ebooks Are Another Technology Shift

Just as the Internet introduced both competition for existing library services and openings for new library ones, the introduction of ebooks presents additional opportunities for competition with and by libraries. The impact on libraries will be uneven, because libraries deliver value in so many ways. The survival of libraries will depend on their ability to take advantage of ebook technologies to deliver new kinds of value, even as competition arises in the delivery of their traditional services.

The shift to ebook delivery presents a variety of challenges for libraries. They'll have to figure out how to manage ebook reading devices, reader application software, rights management, and licensing. An even larger challenge will be learning how to work alongside publishers and distribution channels to make it as easy for patrons to use ebooks as it is for them to use print books today. Needless to say, there's a lot of work to do, and it's not entirely clear how this work will be supported.

Nurturing Ebook Culture

Public libraries will find themselves competing with fresh players on multiple fronts, even as they deal with budget cuts and scramble for funding. The economic efficiencies that spring from library lending of print don't easily transfer to ebooks. Ebook business models that replace library lending will enable publishers to capture value directly. For example, direct-to-consumer ebook subscription services may compete directly with lending services offered through libraries.

It would be tragic if communities found themselves divided between ebook-haves and ebook-have-nots.

Public libraries also serve their communities as physical gathering places that nurture culture. But libraries have no monopoly on offering free Wi-Fi Internet and comfortable reading and cultural spaces; it's only a matter of time before Starbucks and others add free ebooks, book clubs, and other content services onto the music and news that they currently offer. Bookstores of all types will not want to be left out of the reading-room market.

It's unlikely, however, that the Starbucks and Borders of the world are going to want to serve the folks who can't afford the $3 lattes or the $20 hardcovers. It would be tragic if communities found themselves divided between ebook-haves and ebook-have-nots.

A Deluge of Digitization

No one doubts the worth of a great academic library; libraries have long been used as recruiting tools for both faculty and students and given buildings designed by famous architects. They've been building up their book collections for years, and having these books creates a competitive advantage for the institution. Mass book digitization changes that profoundly. People don't care where an ebook is, as long as they can read it.

Most prominent among organizations that have recognized the value of turning academic library volumes into ebooks is Google, with its Google Books service. A key component of the settlement of Google's lawsuit with publishers and authors is an institutional subscription service. Even if the settlement is not approved by the court, expect Google Editions and other digitized-book services, such as the Internet Archive's Open Library, to offer world-class book collections at prices that mid-size and small libraries can afford. There's no reason such services wouldn't be offered directly to individuals as well. These services will compete directly with the print book collections of academic libraries, and libraries will need to reconcile their educational missions with updated roles as subscription administrators, just as they have done with e-journals.

The cheap distribution channels made possible by ebooks will allow libraries to nurture written scholarship in ways that were not possible with print. Cheap digitization will allow libraries to expand the reach of collections, while lowered barriers to publication will help libraries foster written scholarship into the future.

Now more than ever, children need to learn how to find, access, evaluate, and interact with digital information.

Teaching Students About Ebooks

School librarians may well find their space, print collections, and budgets completely devoured by an ebook monster sooner than they imagine; we are only a few years away from ebook reader devices being cheap enough that it will be economically feasible to put an entire school library and all of a school's textbooks into every student's backpack. This could be mortal competition for school libraries as such.

Or maybe not. Now more than ever, children need to learn how to find, access, evaluate, and interact with digital information. Devices don't make that happen by themselves, even if they come with thousands of carefully selected ebooks.

Participate!

These issues stand to alter the face of school, public, and college library service. . . .

Obviously, there is still a lot of uncertainty about how and when libraries develop ebook services as well as how libraries might best fit in a world where books are mostly consumed via ebook readers. What seems clear is that if libraries just sit back and wait to see what happens, rather than participating in the cycle of innovation and competition, they will end up with diminished roles in our culture. It's important that we don't let that happen.

7

Publishers and Libraries Need to Adapt to the Demands of E-book Readers

Dan Tonkery

An expert on online publishing, Dan Tonkery is the founder and senior executive for Content Strategies, a company that advises small or not-for-profit publishing houses on marketing strategies and actively assists in the buying and selling of informational databases.

The Apple iPad and other tablet devices are revolutionizing how consumers experience and interact with print media. Publishers cannot lag in adapting their print-based texts to mobile devices. Not only do these companies need to get their publications online (possibly to save their businesses), they must also understand that new applications (apps) are needed to make their content fit the reading habits of the more technology-savvy users. The same advice holds true for libraries. These institutions must adapt to the demands of electronic book and newspaper readers; they must find ways to make library databases accessible to patrons equipped with electronic readers. Simply translating printed text to electronic text will not be enough; libraries and publishers will be compelled to offer engaging applications appropriate for electronic tablets or suffer a decline in patrons and customers.

Dan Tonkery, "The iPad and Its Possible Impact on Publishers and Libraries," *Searcher: The Magazine for Database Professionals*, vol. 18, no. 8, October 2010, pp. 39–42. Copyright © 2010 by Searcher. All rights reserved. Reproduced by permission of Information Today, Inc., www.infotoday.com.

In early April 2010, Apple introduced its much anticipated iPad, a launch that has set the consumer electronics market on fire. The iPad looks like an iPhone on steroids. It is about the size of a book, half-an-inch thick with a 9.7" color screen, and has a battery life of 10 hours. It runs all of the applications (apps) for the iPhone or iPod Touch and works well as an ebook reader. The apps business is a large part of the appeal for the iPad and iPhone. With an app, one has a customized program that performs a customized function. Apple has just surpassed 10,000 native apps for the iPad. At this rate of development, one can predict nearly 100,000 apps for the iPad by the end of the year, with a third of the apps dedicated to gaming.

By the end of May, Apple had sold more than 2,000,000 iPads with 1,000,000-plus bought sight unseen. Apple devotees buy whatever Apple produces apparently. The iPad first launched in the U.S. and recently began selling in most major international markets. Eager buyers around the world stood in line all night to be one of the first to get their hands on this new product.

So after 2 months, what was the market reaction to its new purchases? Have Apple followers been taken in by Apple's slick marketing or does this device meet expectations? The answer is simple. The iPad has far exceeded everyone's expectations including Apple's! While the first release does not include all the features that some might want, Apple has another hit on its hands.

Tablet computing has found a definite place in our society.

Tablet computing has found a definite place in our society. I don't think that computer manufacturers are worried about the iPad replacing their sales of PCs and laptops. Today, the sales ratio between the PC and iPad is about 60-to-1. Most computer sales are replacements for existing equipment. Within 5 years, the tablet computer sales ratio has been predicted to climb to a 5-1 ratio. Hand-held devices, including smartphones, tablet computers, and e-readers, are the fastest-growing section of the computing market.

The Blossoming Ebook Market

When you add the 2,000,000-plus iPads, the strong sales of the Kindle e-reader from Amazon, the Barnes & Noble's Nook, plus another 20 e-readers hitting the market by the end of December 2010, you see why book publishers are excited about the electronic book marketplace. In the first quarter of this year, sales of ebooks by the major distributors exceeded $91 million. To put those ebook sales in perspective, Barnes & Noble's store sales for the same time period were down 5.5%, and Borders' sales were down 11%. The brick-and-mortar bookstores continue to see a decline in print sales; the only bright spot is the ebook consumer market, in which sales are skyrocketing. Amazon's $9.99 ebook pricing has ignited sales in the ebook market.

After the resolution of some pricing issues between Amazon and a few major publishers, ebook prices began rising. Perhaps a better business model has developed for the publishers, but consumers still are getting a good deal. Apple opened its own ebookstore, iBooks, and has sold 5,000,000 ebooks during the first 2 months of the iPad. Both Barnes & Noble and Borders have released iPad apps so that users who have bought books for their e-readers can read the book on an iPad. Although the Kindle remains Amazon's e-reader of choice, it also offers free Kindle apps for the PC, Mac, iPhone, and iPad. A wise move. Maybe the serious reader will remain with the Kindle, but most of my friends have eagerly dumped their Kindles for the iPad because the iPad has so much more to offer. The competition between Amazon and Apple may not be over, however. Rumors circulate that new versions of the Kindle may have a lot more tablet computing features.

Ebooks can be delivered from a server to any person or place around the globe in seconds.

Having widespread availability and support for e-readers opens up the international market for ebooks. While not the subject of this article, an international market for ebooks opens up the issue of international rights. In the past, the book industry worked on selling and maintaining rights at a geographic level. Authors' books are sold around the world under strict rights involving various publishers. That entire rights industry must rethink their decades-old contracts. Ebooks can be delivered from a server to any person or place around the globe in seconds. At a recent meeting in New York City, the DigitalBook 2010, one vendor reported delivering ebooks to 170 different countries from an analysis of one day's sales. Clearly the ebook world distribution system is going to challenge the traditional rights and permissions area of publishing to develop a new system of rights.

Newspapers Reinvent Themselves

The newspaper industry is another sector of the publishing community looking at the iPad and other tablet computers to save their market. The plight of the newspaper industry has been well-chronicled during the past few years. With the growth of free online news channels, circulation levels of newspapers around the world have been dropping. Staff reductions, mergers, bankruptcies from the loss of advertising dollars are commonplace. In a recent study by OECD [Organization for Economic Co-operation and Development], 20 out of 30 OECD countries are facing continuing declining newspaper circulations. In the period 2007–2009 circulation in the U.S. declined 30%; in the U.K., 25%; in Greece, 20%; in

Italy, 18%; and in Canada, 17%. Advertising amounts for 87% of the revenue for U.S. newspapers. In the U.S., *The New York Times* says about 70% of its online readers are subscribers to its print edition. Yet few readers have been willing to pay for online news.

The New York Times and other major newspapers are still trying to find business models that will recapture lost advertising dollars or convince readers to pay for news content. Is the iPad the magic bullet? In the 2 short months, several newspapers have received good feedback on their iPad edition. *USA TODAY* is the top app downloaded in the free category; the FT [*Financial Times*] has gotten great reviews. Users like the iPad version of the FT much better than the online version. *The [Boston] Globe* has been well-received.

It is too early to predict if the iPad will be able to save the newspaper industry.

It is too early to predict if the iPad will be able to save the newspaper industry but there are a number of iPad design companies available to develop apps for newspaper publishers that capture the functionality of the iPad. One thing is clear to every one: Simply putting a print-centric version of the newspaper online, an app that just mimics the print, is a non-starter.

Part of the problem that newspapers have is the lack of vision at the top. I have read a number of critics on the newspaper industry and they are calling for a change in leadership. Appoint a digital format editor and a print editor. The versions are two different animals and require different styles. In the online world, most newspaper applications are simply too print-centric, PDF versions of the printed newspaper. The iPad is a different platform and requires creativity to gain the user's attention. Something other than stale news is required to get a user to open his or her pocketbook and actually pay for news.

While the iPad may not be the magic bullet, most users believe that this New Age machine is magic in its design. The best examples of magic in publishing have been in the apps for the magazine publishers. For my money, the app for *Wired* magazine from Conde Nast is well worth the $4.99. Other readers think so as well. Conde reported that it had 73,000 downloads for the first issue, a number almost equal to newsstand sales. Of course, many of *Wired*'s readers are techies or technology followers, so their success may not be repeatable. However, it is clear that by applying creativity in using the iPad as a tool with many features, one can develop apps that are not just a stack of banners with a few videos exported from a paper layout program. *Popular Science* had 34,000 downloads and is another model of what can be achieved with an iPad.

Electronic Readers for the Classroom

The next area of the publishing world taking notice of the iPad is textbook publishers. The high cost of textbooks has been a hot topic for several years. Congress has even taken up the issue. The governor of California recently announced that the state of California was switching over to etextbooks, seen as lowercost alternatives. Not only is the cost of printing and distributing textbooks expensive, but the update cycle is slow. Publishers lose massive amounts of revenue through the used textbook market. Follett, the largest college bookstore operator, is also the largest reseller of textbooks. Used books have a higher profit margin than new, but the publisher loses the revenue on the used book sale.

Follett operates Cafescribe, an etextbook site, and Coursesmart operates the largest etextbook site with more than 8,000 books from many major publishers. The iPad offers greater enhancement features over the standard etextbook. Developers have an opportunity to develop new products that take advantage of the iPad features and other tablet computer capabilities. Think of how one could integrate etextbooks with lecture notes on major chapters, or watch a video of an experiment, or take an interactive exam. The textbook can become an integrated product with sound, video, 3D models, etc. Developers have barely begun to explore the features of the new platform.

Publishers must seek out iPad design companies that can build iPad apps from the ground up.

New Thinking, New Applications

Publishers must seek out iPad design companies that can build iPad apps from the ground up. Taking the data from old paper layout programs and just repositioning it is not a sellable alternative. Producing a print-centric app is doomed to failure. Few users or advertisers are going to pay for a simple dressed-up product. In most online applications, publishers took the old print publications, put a little lipstick and eye shadow on their pit bull, and tried to convince everyone that they had a shiny new product. Maybe the technology would only support that level of improvement back in the days of the early web, but now we have the iPad and tablet computing as tools to achieve something new and exciting.

To make the transition from a printed product to an e-product that works in a tablet environment requires radical, out-of-the-box thinking. There is a general philosophy that if a publisher can enhance the ebook in various ways, then the publisher should be able to keep the public paying print book prices for content. A number of publishers are already working on educating staffs on the enhancing of the ebook. There is a partnership between the Idea Logical Company and Digital Book World, the unit of F+W Media, to produce a series of nine webinars on the topic of enhancing ebooks. E2BU

[Enhanced Ebook University] will produce a series of nine webinars on various aspects of the book enhancement process.

The iPad, the iPhone, and a number of other smartphones are the first of a long line of mobile computing devices that have the potential to radically change our world from the era of the web browser into apps on mobile devices. That transition from a world dominated by browser-based information to apps on mobile devices is a fundamental change in our use of the internet. Already social networking sites such as Facebook have made a serious dent in traditional email traffic and the time that users stay online. Users are spending their time online in different ways than they have in the past, and this should send a strong message to publishers and libraries.

To maintain its position on campus, the library needs to pressure database vendors and library system suppliers to support the new mobile computing environment.

Libraries Need to Embrace the Change

For libraries, the introduction of the iPad is both exciting and challenging. Mobile computing with the BlackBerry or smartphone has given some insight into user behavior. The introduction of the iPad and its competitors will have a serious impact on library services. The widespread availability of online resources in nearly every discipline, powerful search tools, and discovery services have all contributed to the library's loss of importance on campus. Recent surveys by Ithaka and the Center for Studies in Higher Education at University of California–Berkeley paint a grim picture for the future of the library. There is a continuing decline in using the library as the entry point in starting a research project. Faculty depends on the library to buy and provide access to material and still see that as an important role.

To maintain its position on campus, the library needs to pressure database vendors and library system suppliers to support the new mobile computing environment. Students may not clamor to use the online catalog on their iPhone, but expect them to realize the need to support the iPad. The databases that the library buys from EBSCO, Gale, or ProQuest should be redeveloped for the iPad and other mobile computing devices.

Recently at the Medical Library Association, I had an opportunity to review Unbound Medicine's iPad edition of a number of reference books in pharmacology. The early versions are impressive and show how mobile computing might work in a hospital or laboratory environment. One can only imagine how these applications would work if designed to utilize the full functions of the iPad or other tablet computers. For now, companies can only take the data supplied by the publisher, but soon we should see reference books that have been built not on print-centric data but as new works integrated with a range of media.

We are on the edge of a digital revolution. Apple with its iPad has lifted the veil of darkness, and everyone is getting a quick peek into a future that extends far beyond print-centric products. The technology and communications, standards, and user demand are there for us to move light years forward. We are bound only by our own creativity.

8

Libraries Need to Ask Tough Questions Before Embracing E-books

Meredith Farkas

Meredith Farkas is the head of instructional services at Portland State University in Oregon and an adjunct faculty member at San Jose State University's School of Library and Information Science. When she wrote this piece, she was head of instructional initiatives at Norwich University in Vermont. She is also the author of Social Software in Libraries: Building Collaboration, Communication and Community Online *and a monthly columnist for* American Libraries *magazine.*

Most librarians recognize that electronic books will become a significant part of public and academic library collections, but challenges remain as to how libraries and e-book providers can adapt to each other's needs. Libraries must take part in resolving the most pertinent concerns. For example, electronic collections are virtual, thus the library gains nothing but access for its investment. This means libraries do not "own" what they pay for, and unlike physical books, libraries often have trouble lending e-books to patrons or loaning them to distant users through interlibrary loan. In fact, traditional lending models fail, requiring e-book providers and libraries to work together to devise a system that will meet patrons' demands. Access is another major stumbling block because digital rights' issues and the incompatibility of e-book providers' databases make it difficult to get pa-

trons the works they need. Although it is clear that e-books are here to stay, libraries must face these challenges head-on and make decisions based on what will best serve their patrons.

I really like eBooks, which is something that surprised me when I won my Kindle last Spring in a raffle. In fact, just about every book I've read since then has been on my Kindle or occasionally on my husband's iPad (I greatly prefer reading on the Kindle). When I first assumed I would hate reading ebooks, I'd based it on the experiences I'd had reading books on my computer through academic platforms like NetLibrary and eBrary. Reading on the Kindle is nothing like that—the absence of a glossy backlit screen is key for me. And the consumer ebook market seems to have exploded in just the past six months, even for those who are far from early adopters. When my dad got a Kindle in September I knew eBook readers had arrived. Even at Norwich I'm starting to get inquiries from patrons about whether they can read ebooks from the library on their mobile devices. There's no doubt at this point: Ebooks do have a real place in the future of reading. Unfortunately, the way most people are using eBooks at this point completely bypasses the library, and this is what publishers and ebook manufacturers seem to want. Why wouldn't they?

I am deeply concerned about the fact that many libraries are increasing their collections of ebooks to the point where a huge chunk of their collection development purchases are ebooks.

Concerns About Ebooks for Libraries

And the options that libraries now have for ebooks (in terms of content, interface, interoperability, etc.) are, by and large, piss-poor. I am deeply concerned about the fact that many libraries are increasing their collections of ebooks to the point where a huge chunk of their collection development purchases are ebooks. They provide a compelling model. In many cases, multiple students can read the same book at once. The books take less time and effort in terms of processing and take up no physical space at all. But the negatives, the uncertainties of where the ebook market is headed, and the current restrictions most ebook vendors have placed on their products often outweigh the benefits. That doesn't mean we can bury our heads in the sand and ignore this huge trend, but I also agree strongly with Eli Neiburger at the *Library Journal* eBook Summit that libraries are screwed.

This post is basically a stream of consciousness outline of some of the concerns that have been swirling around in my head regarding ebooks. I am far from an ebook expert. I don't read contracts from vendors and I don't know the ins and outs of the ebook market, DRM [digital rights management] first sale doctrine, etc. I'm just someone in charge of collection development for our largest school who realizes how little most librarians know about what we're getting into with ebooks (me included) and who is really concerned about where things are going. . . .

Getting an ebook on my Kindle is ridiculously simple. . . . Getting an ebook from a library is often a circuitous and confusing process.

No Incentive to Work with Libraries

Buying a physical book versus checking it out from the library are not radically different processes. Both have very small barriers (leaving the house to get a library book or buy a book at a bookstore vs. waiting at least a day or more to get a book purchased online). Getting an ebook on my Kindle is ridiculously simple. Click on the order button and it's there. Heck, I can even preview part of the first chapter for free to see if I want to buy it! And for the average person who just wants to read a book and be done with it, they don't care about it working on other devices, any restrictions on lending, etc. Getting an ebook from a library is often a circuitous and confusing process; so confusing that libraries have to create tutorials on how to do it. This doesn't even take into account the myriad interoperability issues when patrons want to actually read a library ebook on their mobile/ereader device. And the fact that libraries often can't get ebook packages/options that provide the content our patrons want (especially in academic libraries). The worst part is that I can't see this getting better in the future when it makes no financial sense for Amazon, B&N [Barnes & Noble], Sony, etc. to make it easy for libraries to get and provide this content to their patrons. If the e-reader providers largely control the market for ebooks, libraries will be aced out.

In a perfect world, we'd have a collection of ebooks that were all accessible through a single easy-to-use, easy-to-search platform. Unfortunately, that doesn't look like it'll ever happen.

Interlibrary loan [ILL] is an important part of what we do. Many consortia have cooperative collection development agreements where they will not duplicate collections and can borrow from each other. What does that mean when what they're buying are ebooks? Only a small number of ebook vendors (actually, Springer is the only one I know of) allow for any sort of ILL, which means that the more our book collections go digital, the less we will be able to loan to other libraries or borrow from other libraries. That libraries are going in this direction without considering the impact on ILL are really shooting ourselves, our patrons, our profession, in the foot. Just try to imagine your library without interlibrary loan. I know I can't.

Incompatible Databases

In a perfect world, we'd have a collection of ebooks that were all accessible through a single easy-to-use, easy-to-search platform. Unfortunately, that doesn't look like it'll ever happen. The best we can do is to make our ebook collections findable via our library catalog, but that lacks the sophisticated search functionality of the individual platforms themselves. I teach our distance learners how to search for books in the catalog *and* eBrary, even though our catalog contains the eBrary MARC [machine-readable cataloging] records. Why? Because the search functionality of eBrary is better. eBrary can search the full-text of books and will often pull up a much better results list.

We get a lot of Gale's literature reference works through Literature Resource Center [LRC]. However, LRC doesn't contain all of Gale's literature reference works, and if you want to subscribe to those, you can't get it on the same platform as the LRC. For example, we want to get Gale's Children's Literature Review since English majors seem to have increasing interest in research[ing] YA [young adult] authors. Given the size of the collection (well over 100 volumes) and the direction that reference collections are going in, it made sense to look into getting it online. The problem is, we can't get this collection through Literature Resource Center. Instead, we would need to catalog it and hope that users stumble upon it. We teach English students to search MLA [Modern Language Association] International Bibliography and Literature Resource Center. We teach them about our print reference works. We teach students how to find books of criticism on specific works or authors in the catalog. Now, we need to somehow explain that while most of our reference collection lives on the first floor of the library, some of it is online and accessible through the catalog if you know the specific title of the work (since it's not like you could do a search for Roald Dahl in the catalog and have the Children's Literature Review pop up).

This was difficult enough for me to explain in a blog post for librarians; just imagine me trying to explain all this to a bunch of Freshmen in our EN 102 classes!

Difficult to Browse

Browsing is still an important part of the discovery experience. Every time I am helping a student find books on a specific topic, I will suggest that they look to the left and right of the books they are specifically looking for on the shelf to see if there's something that didn't come up in our search that would be a great fit for their research. There's nothing like serendipity, and serendipitous browsing is still not replicated well online. And this becomes even more difficult to imagine replicating when you have a mix of ebook collections and print books. The collection becomes even more fragmented, even more difficult to browse.

Differing Rights' Protections

I always feel embarrassed when I have to explain to our distance learners that they can't do any of the things they'd like to do with eBrary books. Our distance learners are often on the road for their work. Many are deployed in Iraq and Afghanistan and have Internet access for very limited periods of time. I even had a student on a submarine who had 1 hour per day to access the Internet and get all of the work that requires an Internet connection done. So when I tell them, no, you can't download the books; no, you can't print more than a small portion of any book; no, you can't read them offline, I feel like a jerk. Why are we providing such a crappy product to our students that doesn't meet their needs in any way, shape or form?

And of course eBrary says that their DRM is absolutely necessary to protect the copyright holders, but then you have a platform like eBook Library, where users can download books using Adobe Digital Editions where the document will simply expire after a predetermined amount of time. There are ways to protect copyright holders and still provide ebooks in a way that works for most users. From what I've seen (which isn't a lot), eBook Library so far has come the closest to providing the sort of user experience my students need. But, of course, the more platforms you purchase or lease access to books on, the more different rules and restrictions they will have. And patrons won't understand why you can download this ebook, but not this one, or why this one will let you print, but this other one will stop you at 5 pages.

The issue of accessibility . . . is a huge legal issue that too few librarians think about on a regular basis.

Then you add in the nightmare that is ensuring that ebooks work on mobile devices and dedicated e-readers. There are different formats, different constraints. Then you bring in the issue of accessibility, which is a huge legal issue that too few librarians think about on a regular basis. And not knowing where the ebook market is going and what devices patrons will own in the future, makes it difficult to make any decisions now. But at the same time, can libraries afford to sit and wait until there's greater clarity regarding the future of books?

Access but Not Ownership

When my library buys 20 physical books, we own those books. Those books don't disappear unless a patron loses them (in which case we usually recoup our costs) or we choose to remove the book from the collection. We can ILL those books, we can put them on reserve, and there are no further costs for that book (unless it requires rebinding) beyond the initial purchase. But take a look at our eBrary collection. We pay lots of money each year for access to tens of thousands of books but we don't own anything. We cancel our subscription and those books are gone. Books get added and disappear from our eBrary collection depending on their current deals with publishers, meaning that something a student used for their research two months ago may not actually be in our collection when they are looking to cite something from it.

Then there are ebook collections that libraries have perpetual access to. For those, we usually have to pay a platform fee each year to keep our access to that book. We can't just mount it on our own servers. Some vendors, like eBook Library allow you to archive your own copy, but I'm not really sure what that means since it's not like we can then email copies of it to students or just put it up on our server for anyone to download. If eBook Library fails, I'm not sure how we would make those books we "own" accessible. I know that some vendors belong to Portico and that Portico has now opened up a separate ebook preservation initiative [which electronically preserves titles that may go out of print], but the majority of ebook vendors we would want to work with are not currently members. I'm not an expert in this area by any stretch of the imagination and I've never read over every detail of the contracts we have with these vendors, but I am concerned that some librarians may not be thinking about the long-term preservation of the ebooks they are purchasing.

We pay lots of money each year for access to tens of thousands of books but we don't own anything.

Librarians Are Still Needed

I can't tell you how many articles I've read recently about patron-driven acquisitions and the vast majority have been entirely positive, raising no concerns whatsoever about the practice. I'm not saying I think it's a bad idea, but I don't think it's the magic bullet that many are making it out to be.

Collection development is a tricky game. It's not just about building a collection for the people who use it today, but anticipating what people might want in the future. For example, my library had a rather poor Chinese history collection. Then we got a Chinese major, a professor to teach Chinese history, and the possibility of a Chinese studies major starting next year. Suddenly, in one year, I had to put a tremendous amount of my social sciences collection budget towards filling in that area. Right now at Norwich, Latin American history is not a hot area of study, but I still make an effort to buy some of the best works in the area. There has to be a balance struck. Obviously, you are going to spend more on areas that people are studying now, but you have to keep an eye on creating a balance that recognizes that hot areas of study change over time.

Collection development is a tricky game. It's not just about building a collection for the people who use it today, but anticipating what people might want in the future.

We actually did patron-driven acquisitions for our distance learners for a few years. Instead of doing ILL for our students who live all over the world, we purchased whatever they wanted. After two years, I looked at the books that had been purchased in the first year and found that only two of them had circulated more than that first time. We now have large collections of books on Zulu warfare and the military history of Australia because two students were interested in those subjects, but will those ever get used again? It's highly unlikely. Just because one student is interested in a specific book or topic doesn't mean that others will be. I'm not saying that purchasing some books that students want [doesn't make] sense, but having seen what a 100% patron-driven acquisitions model looks like, I don't think it solves any problems.

Look, I get it. We're in a tough spot. We're trying to do more with less. We're trying to justify continued funding in the face of the fact that such a small proportion of what we buy gets used *now*. But I'm not sure that moving a large portion of our acquisitions budget to patron-driven acquisitions is a responsible decision in the long-run. I do think putting some of a library's collection budget towards patron-driven acquisitions is an excellent idea and that's what we're experimenting with this semester with eBook Library. But I still feel in my bones that it would do a disservice to the long-term health of the collection to rely solely on the taste of today's patrons. To me, cooperative collection development is a model for sustainable collection-building that makes much more sense.

I don't know where ebooks, patron-driven acquisitions, or e-readers are going. When I read posts [about ebooks], I wonder if reading online in the future will not resemble in any way what we do and use for it today. It seriously hurts my brain to even imagine what reading will look like 10–20 years from now. What I do know is that the more I read about ebooks and the future of publishing, the more concerned I get. And the more I talk to librarians about this the more I realize how little many of us think about any of the larger issues (beyond content and perhaps accessibility) when we think about getting ebook collections. I actually saw a forum post in response to my *American Libraries* column about the Terms of Service regarding Kindle books that they didn't sign any agreement when they bought a Kindle for their library. Sigh. . . . People with very little understanding of these issues (and I include myself in that group) are making big decisions for libraries. Ebooks can no longer be the realm of knowledge of just a few experts; we *all* need to understand the current issues, keep up with new writing on the subject (from librarians, educators, technologists and the publishing/e-reader/mobile device world), and scan the horizon to gain some sense of where things are going. Otherwise, how can we possibly make collection decisions about these materials? Whether we want to make those decisions or not, they are going to be continuously foisted on us over time. I had a faculty member last semester ask if we could get the *Encyclopedia of Associations* online instead of in print. Our patrons are going to increasingly come to us with e-readers that they got for the holidays or their birthday, wanting to see what the library is offering that they can read on their shiny new device. Whether we want to face it or not, we owe it to our patrons and the future of our libraries to learn as much as we can about this stuff so that we can make decisions that best serve the patrons and the institution.

9

Electronic Readers Are More Environmentally Friendly than Print Books

Brian Palmer

Brian Palmer writes chiefly on environmental topics for Slate *magazine and the* Washington Post.

Although electronic book readers require some rare metals and toxic elements to manufacture and produce greenhouse gas emissions in the manufacturing process, overall these devices will lower the average consumer's carbon footprint when compared with buying hardbound books. Traditional book publishing uses lots of resources, espeically paper and water. E-book creation uses far fewer resources. The bookselling market also produces a lot of waste in terms of returned and unused copies that often end up in landfills. E-books have no waste. Because of these savings, experts estimate that electronic reading devices earn back their carbon investments somewhere around the twentieth e-book a consumer purchases.

Environmental analysis can be an endless balancing of this vs. that. Do you care more about conserving water or avoiding toxic chemical usage? Minimizing carbon dioxide emissions or radioactive nuclear waste? But today the [*Washington Post* column the Green] Lantern has good news: There will be no Sophie's Choice [a difficult choice between two loves] when it comes to ebooks. As long as you consume a healthy number of titles, you read at a normal pace and you don't trade in your gadget every year, perusing electronically will lighten your environmental impact.

If the Lantern has taught you anything, it's that most consumer products make their biggest scar on the Earth during manufacture and transport, before they ever get into your greedy little hands. Accordingly, green-minded consumers are usually—although not always—better off buying fewer things when possible. Reusable cloth diapers, for example, are better than disposables, because the environmental costs of manufacture and transport outweigh those of washing.

Every time you download and read an electronic book, rather than purchasing a new pile of paper, you're paying back a little bit of the carbon dioxide and water deficit from the Kindle production process.

Ebooks Use Fewer Resources

Think of an e-reader as the cloth diaper of books. Sure, producing one Kindle is tougher on the environment than printing a single paperback copy of "Pride and Prejudice." But every time you download and read an electronic book, rather than purchasing a new pile of paper, you're paying back a little bit of the carbon dioxide and water deficit from the Kindle production process. The actual operation of an e-reader represents a small percentage of its total environmental impact, so if you run your device into the ground, you'll end up paying back that debt many times over. (Unless, of course, reading "Pride and Prejudice" over and over again is enough for you. Then, by all means, buy it in print and enjoy.)

Let's talk numbers. According to the environmental consulting firm Cleantech, which aggregated a series of studies, a single book generates about 7.5 kilograms (almost 17 pounds) of carbon dioxide equivalents. (That's the value of all its greenhouse gas emissions expressed in terms of the impact of carbon dioxide.) This figure includes production, transport and either recycling or disposal.

Earning Back E-reader Carbon Emissions

Apple's iPad generates 130 kilograms of carbon dioxide equivalents during its lifetime, according to company estimates. Amazon has not released numbers for the Kindle, but Cleantech and other analysts put it at 168 kilograms. Those analyses do not indicate how much additional carbon is generated per book read (as a result of the energy required to host the e-bookstore's servers and power the screen while you read), but they do include the full cost of manufacture, which likely accounts for the lion's share of emissions. (The iPad uses just three watts of electricity while you're reading, far less than most light bulbs.) If we can trust those numbers, then, the iPad pays for its CO_2 emissions about one-third of the way through your 18th book. You'd need to get halfway into your 23rd book on Kindle to get out of the environmental red.

The average user purchases three books per month. At that rate, you could earn back your iPad's carbon dioxide in just six months.

So far, electronic readers—not the machines, in this case, but their owners—seem to be in a hurry to get out of that red zone. Forrester Research estimates that the average user purchases three books per month. At that rate, you could earn back your iPad's carbon dioxide in just six months.

Water is also a major consideration. The U.S. newspaper and book publishing industries together consume 153 billion gallons of water annually, according to figures by the non-profit group Green Press Initiative included in the Cleantech analysis. It takes about seven gallons to produce the average printed book, while e-publishing companies can create a digital book with less than two cups of water. (Like any other company, ebook publishers consume water through the paper they use and other office activities.) Researchers estimate that 79 gallons of water are needed to make an e-reader. So you come out on top, water-wise, after reading about a dozen books.

E-readers also have books beat on toxic chemicals. The production of ink for printing releases a number of volatile organic compounds into the atmosphere, including hexane, toluene and xylene, which contribute to smog and asthma. Some of them may also cause cancer or birth defects. Computer production is not free of hard-to-pronounce chemicals, to be sure, but both the iPad and the Kindle comply with Europe's RoHS [Restriction of Hazardous Substances] standards, which ban some of the scarier chemicals that have been involved in electronics production. E-readers do, however, require the mining of nonrenewable minerals, such as columbite-tantalite, which sometimes come from politically unstable regions. And experts can't seem to agree on whether we're at risk of exhausting the world's supply of lithium, the lifeblood of the e-reader's battery.

Between a quarter and a third of a bookstore's volumes will ultimately be shipped back to the publisher and on to recycling centers or landfills.

Use Libraries and Online Bookstores

If you're not ready to plunk down $139 for a Kindle or $499 for an iPad, or if you just love the feel of dead tree between your fingers, there's one thing you can do to significantly ease the environmental impact of your reading: Buy your books online. Brick-and-mortar bookstores are very inefficient because they stock way more books than they can sell. Between a quarter and a third of a bookstore's volumes will ultimately be shipped back to the publisher and on to recycling centers or landfills.

An even better option is to walk to your local library, which can spread the environmental impact of a single book over an entire community. Unfortunately, libraries are underutilized. Studies suggest that fewer than a third of Americans visit their local library at least once a month, and fewer than half went in the last year. Libraries report that the average community member checks out 7.4 books per year—far less than the three per month consumed on e-readers—and more than a third of those items were children's books.

Of course, you could also stop reading altogether. But then how would you know how much carbon you saved?

10

Books Are an Expendable Format, but Long-Form Writing Must Continue

Diane Wachtell

Diane Wachtell is the executive director of the New Press, a not-for-profit publisher in New York. She has published articles on the publishing industry and its future in the Chronicle of Higher Education, Publishers Weekly, *and* Counterpunch.

Books are simply packages for the underlying, long-form texts that reside within. Society can live without books, but it cannot survive without the ideas conveyed in well-executed, well-researched long-form writing. Publishers have long understood that long-form writing is an investment. Publishers must pay for authors to develop these ideas and for the staff to edit the resulting text and make it ready for publication. This takes time and money. Electronic publishing poses a certain threat to this type of writing: By supposedly giving anyone the ability to produce and disseminate a written text, the investment in and nurturing of ideas will diminish. The race to put anything out in electronic format will ensure that fewer instances of carefully crafted and edited long-form writing will inhabit a world of unpolished or incomplete texts. Electronic publishers have found a good market in reprinting old titles, but if the industry is to blossom, it must recognize and invest in new long-form works.

In 1980, I dropped out of college and spent a year writing a play about a bibliophile who one day changed course and began to build furniture out of his books. Today, after 25 years in the publishing industry and having edited some 200 works of long-form nonfiction, I continue to see physical books as largely symbolic, aesthetic objects. In my house, they weigh down the corner of a kid's art project or hold up the edge of a shelf.

They are not sacrosanct.

"Books have had a kind of spooky power, embedded as they are in the very structures of learning, commerce, and culture by which we have absorbed, stored, and transmitted information, opinion, art, and wisdom," wrote the acclaimed editor Elisabeth Sifton in a magazine article last year [2009]. But in truth, the books on our library shelves are little more than furniture.

Life on earth would be severely diminished without the well-thought-out, well-researched, written works that communicate expertise, insight, and creative ideas from one human being to another.

We Do Not Need Books, We Need Ideas

And that is why the current attempt to hold a mirror up to the mouth of the book-publishing industry to see if it is still breathing strikes me as misguided. We do not need books. Civil society is not predicated on lovely-to-hold objets d'art that can double as flower presses.

What we cannot survive without is ideas. Life on earth would be severely diminished without the well-thought-out, well-researched, written works that communicate expertise, insight, and creative ideas from one human being to another. That, historically, has been the role of books, and they have played it admirably, in works from the Bible to *Uncle Tom's Cabin* to *Silent Spring* and *The Shock Doctrine*.

In our angst about the Kindle and the iPad, we are conflating the "how" of written works with the "what": We are mistaking the package for the thing itself. What would be terribly frightening to lose is not the book per se but the tradition of long-form texts—call them "lofties"—that for centuries have been the primary vehicle through which creative, illuminating, controversial, and important ideas have been communicated. What is crucial at a time when habits of consumption are changing—for reasons both economic and technological—is to ensure the future of lofty ideas, whether they are set in Bodoni or pixels, hand-sewn at the binding or back-lit and scrolled.

Investing in Long-Form Writing

Lisa Dodson spent eight years interviewing low-wage workers and their managers. She raised money to underwrite her travels and research, which included interviews with 800 people from three sectors of the American economy (retail, education, and health care) where middle-class managers interact on a daily basis with the working poor.

Though she set out to write about low-income workers, Dodson heard in her research a bigger story, one that took many years to draw out. When middle-class managers have firsthand contact with ill-paid workers, they have epiphanies about the fundamental unfairness of the American economy, and—here's the riveting part—begin to subvert the system. They bend the rules, pad paychecks, falsify time sheets, and ignore eligibility requirements for treatments and special services on behalf of the workers they supervise. In short, they refuse to be complicit with a set of rules they have come to see as wrong.

Dodson is a sociologist, not a journalist, so her first draft of *The Moral Underground: How Ordinary Americans Subvert an Unfair Economy*, which took the better part of a year to write, was still a diamond in the rough when I saw it. The concepts were there, but the case studies were not yet pulled together powerfully, and Dodson had yet to figure out how to deal with what we came to call the "underground railroad" question—how to write about subversive and illegal behavior without compromising sources and their methods.

We went through two structural edits before the manuscript was ready to be line-edited for style, and then copy-edited for grammar and consistency. While the copy-editing was under way, Dodson worked on her bibliography, source notes, and methodology chapter, so that other sociologists would know how her research met the standards for the field. We published the book this year, to acclaimed reviews. American University selected it as the text for all incoming freshmen.

Readers might be surprised at how many books begin as ideas in the minds of editors, a part of whose expertise involves understanding the role of long-form writing, assessing gaps in the national discourse, and commissioning works to fill those holes.

Putting aside novels, which (unless you are Joyce Carol Oates) can take many years or a lifetime to complete, I can't help but wonder how many drafts Gunnar Myrdal did of *An American Dilemma* or Frances FitzGerald of *Fire in the Lake*. Did David Riesman's *The Lonely Crowd* come to him as a twitter in his ear, or was some research involved? How about Jared Diamond's *Guns, Germs, and Steel*, or Rebecca Skloot's recent *The Immortal Life of Henrietta Lacks?* I do know that last year's history of the NAACP [National Association for the Advancement of Colored People], *Lift Every Voice*, by Patricia Sullivan, was a decade in the making. And Michelle Alexander gave birth to three children in less time than it took her to produce this year's *The New Jim Crow*.

Long-Form Writing Takes Time

Today's book publishers are cast in the role of dinosaurs—lumbering over the media landscape, unaware of their own imminent extinction. But publishers and editors are acutely aware of the difficult, time-consuming process by which lofty ideas are nurtured and developed. Furthermore, it is the rare lofty idea that is the product of a single mind. Readers might be surprised at how many books begin as ideas in the minds of editors, a part of whose expertise involves understanding the role of long-form writing, assessing gaps in the national discourse, and commissioning works to fill those holes.

Wherever ideas originate, they are often simply the starting point on the long road to a finished book, which typically includes extended conversations and conceptual discussions between author and editor about how the material might best be structured, the project's ideal parameters (knowing what to leave out is often an editor's key contribution), how much background is necessary for lay readers to grasp an argument, and so forth. Manuscripts that arrived in "finished" form typically require at least a line edit and a copy edit to maximize the impact of the underlying ideas, to make them coherent and a pleasure to read.

All this is to say that, however we produce lofties, a wealth of money, time, labor, and expertise goes into the creation of any long-form text worth reading.

All this is to say that, however we produce lofties, a wealth of money, time, labor, and expertise goes into the creation of any long-form text worth reading, well before a single designer, printer, sales rep, or bookstore clerk is paid. Lofty ideas do not come cheap. For all the talk about how the future lies in Kindles or iPads, the Kindle and iPad have yet to bring into existence a single lofty idea that did not already exist elsewhere. If downloads are to supersede printed books as successive generations migrate to newer media, the key question is not "Is the book dead?" It is "Who will pay for the lofties?"

New Media Needs the Old

Today the new media exist in a symbiotic relationship with the old. The one cannot survive without the other. Amazon-.com, which developed the Kindle, accounts for almost 20 percent of the sale of the printed editions of most trade books; but publishers create close to 100 percent of books available for Kindle and other e-readers. The three leading electronic purveyors of books—Amazon, Google, and now Apple—are just that . . . purveyors of books.

Unless the new-media mavens take seriously the job of producing new lofty ideas, they will want to come up with a revenue structure for selling e-books that allows traditional publishers to stay in business.

Thus the primary way the electronic triumvirate engages with the publishing industry is by selling old-media products via new media. As a result, most industry conversation continues to be about terms of sale: What is a fair revenue structure for hardcover books sold over the Internet or for downloads of long-form texts? It's like arguing about a fair royalty for audiobooks or whether the unit cost paid to publishers' book-club sales should include the author's share of revenue. Those are important subsidiary-rights issues, to be sure, but nothing in our current conversation speaks to the future of lofty ideas as we know them.

The conversation that is important to our intellectual future has to do with where the germination and cultivation of ideas will reside, and whether that work can or will shift its center of gravity.

For now, e-book companies seem happy to repackage intellectual property. And that is not a bad thing. While the parties involved may argue about how to divide the spoils, almost everyone sees the virtues of increasing access to the world's collective writing—what publishers somewhat prosaically call "the backlist." But creating a virtual "e-Library of Babel" of all books old and new—without opening the discussion of who will bear the costs of creating the long-form texts of the futures—is essentially a new form of cultural appropriation. It does not bode well for the intellectual lives of our grandchildren, who might face a din of undeveloped online manuscripts. Unless the new-media mavens take seriously the job of producing new lofty ideas, they will want to come up with a revenue structure for selling e-books that allows traditional publishers to stay in business.

If, on the other hand, e-retailers deep-six existing publishers by selling lofty ideas at prices that do not cover creation costs, they will lead us to a point where, in the words of the Microsoft partner architect Jaron Lanier in *You Are Not a Gadget: A Manifesto* (Thorndike Press, 2010), "culture is effectively eating its own seed stock." Will the new media take up the mantle of lofty idea creation? The jury is out.

A Culture of Ideas Not Products

Lofty ideas are slow media. They require intensive labor and time, and they are expensive. But they provide the intellectual scaffolding for our national discourse, and are at the heart of our cultural well-being. The standard language of a book contract gives the author final approval of the text but reserves decisions about the jacket and design for the publishing house. That is because the jacket, along with all the other attendant apparatus of book publishing—dingbats, page layouts, point-of-sale displays in bookstores—are acknowledged to be "marketing." They are window dressing to attract attention to an underlying lofty idea that can open the window on to a new way of seeing the world.

We can live without the window dressing, but the world would be a much darker place without the windows.

11

Books Still Matter in a Digital Age

John Donatich

A former vice president of Basic Books, John Donatich is currently the director of Yale University Press. He is also a member of the Council on Foreign Relations and the author of published articles in such periodicals as the Village Voice *and the* Atlantic.

Books have been around for seven centuries. They are portable, accessible collections of knowledge and insight into human thinking. In the digital age, some people accept—even look forward to—the demise of the book. These critics believe written works will rely on concise information packets that will satisfy readers' demands and possibly hyperlink to other topics of related interest. They foresee a universal library of connected thoughts housed ethereally on the Internet, ready for users to log on and get the snippet of knowledge they seek. Such reading habits, though, encourage a different form of learning, one based on skimming that sacrifices context and an understanding of argumentative support of ideas for instant gratification. This may seem a utopian vision to some, but the necessity of long-form writing will never perish. Research, scholarship, and cultural expression will, in many cases, require book-length prose arguments. Even in the age of electronic readers, users still download and access whole books for pleasure and erudition. If society were to scrap the book format, an illiterate and uninformed public would be the unfortunate result.

John Donatich, "Why Books Still Matter," *Journal of Scholarly Publishing*, vol. 40, no. 4, July 2009, pp. 329–342. Copyright © 2009 by the University of Toronto Press. All rights reserved. Reproduced with permission from University of Toronto Press Incorporated (www.utpjournals.com).

Books have a lot of explaining to do these days. Bibliophiles and even publishers are treated with a fair amount of suspicion. Most of us deserve it, as we are apt to carry on like fetishists. You can often hear us gushing over the beautiful object of the book, that 700-year-old feat of perfect engineering. You might see us in raptures over the grain of paper, the pacing of illustrations, the complement of typeface and design. We will bore you with the sensual pleasure of the book: its smell and feel, the way in which a fine book ages. We will study marginalia for its human record, for the physical manifestation of that desire to enter a book, to literally work our way into or impress ourselves onto another's mind.

What could be more human than a book? We speak of its body intimately, name its parts as joints and hinges. How many of us have winced when someone bends a book's covers back sadistically? We call this horrendous act 'breaking the spine.' Yet all of this object love is starting to sound a bit quaint, the sentimental mumblings of Luddites [those who distrust technology] who, on their off hours, argue for the reinstitution of the lyceum, the debating society, and the lecture platform, acting like that certain horse who in 1911 turns his head slowly as he feels the rumbling heat of the Model T Ford bearing down upon him.

Who would have guessed that the latest prediction of the book's demise comes from enthusiasts of the Internet?

Enemies of the Book

But there are more sinister charges against defenders of the book as well. Copyright holders are accused of being enemies of progress and democracy. Libraries groan under the weight of our production; some look forward to the day when we can etherize books online and commit what the director of the Beinecke Library, Frank Turner, calls 'bibliographic euthanasia.'

Those who hate and fear the book have populated its history from the beginning. The banning of books is still a national headline as well as a recent presidential campaign issue. But who would have guessed that the latest prediction of the book's demise comes from enthusiasts of the Internet? One has to wonder why the rhetoric against books has turned so hostile. (Is it because books still matter?) My own personal library does not seek revenge against the Internet, but am I alone in detecting the aggressive tone of those who celebrate the virtual library at the expense of the physical book? Does one technology necessarily obliterate another? Did the television destroy the radio?

It is difficult not to sound threatened when defending the book—especially when the enemies of the book assume that the war is already won. Steve Jobs of Apple recently said that he wasn't even bothering to enter the e-book reader market, because that isn't what the world wants. 'No one reads anymore,' he said. 'It's over.' Several months ago, a *Los Angeles Times* article quoted Markos Moulitsas Zuñiga, founder of the political Web site 'The Daily Kos' who said about those who feared the Google book project, 'like natural selection, there are species that adapt to the changing environment around them and thrive, and others die off.' The article also quotes Stephen Dubner, co-author of the best-selling *Freakonomics*, as saying that

> the crabbiness that emanates from a certain breed of thinker/
> writer ... about how the Internet's cornucopia of informa-
> tion is destroying book culture is based on fear of change
> more than anything. Most people don't even like to change
> the part in their hair; asking them to accept a change in the
> way words are disbursed through culture is a bit much.

Zuñiga adds, 'We no longer have to depend on so-called or self-appointed experts to tell us what we should think.'

So it has really come to this: the day when the self-appointed experts who write books are finally taken down by the self-appointed experts who write blogs. And whom should we trust: the career experts who write books and deliberate over their content while researching for years, or the temporary experts who form the chattering class of the blogosphere? Now, I don't hate blogs or Internet writing. I love them. I read them. I recognize that what goes on in them is different from what goes on in books, and I don't believe that the expansion and growth of the Internet has to mean the death of books.

So it has really come to this: the day when the self-appointed experts who write books are finally taken down by the self-appointed experts who write blogs.

A true confession: I love books more. I always have. As a child, I befuddled and even alarmed my immigrant parents by my affection for books. I took any chance to lose myself in books, though I have always regarded reading as more a kind of engagement than escapism. 'Go outside,' my father would yell at me. During grade school I would sometimes forgo lunch, asking my parents for the twenty-five cents to buy a hot meal while telling the school cafeteria I was going home for lunch. Then I would wait in the woods behind the school during the lunch break, hoarding my change until I had enough to buy a book. When I had collected enough to have a little library, I challenged my sister to blindfold me and test my ability to name a book and its publisher by touch and smell alone. I was right more times than not. A bit obsessive, I agree. Nonetheless, these books awakened in me a tension as a reader: I spent as much time trying to suspend my awareness of the book as a medium and getting lost in the dream of the narrative. I've devoted my entire adult life to publishing, and, despite that, I still think books matter. Or ought to.

A Troubled Future for Books?

However, there is much evidence that points to a troubled future for the book. Here are some statistics:

- The Progress in International Reading Literacy Study reports that reading, writing, and comprehension tests taken by ten-year-old children around the world revealed declining literacy levels. Both the United States and the United Kingdom lost six points in the last five years, ranking respectively number 18 and number 19 globally.

- An NEA [National Education Association] report made national headlines when it revealed that literary reading in America is not only declining rapidly among all groups but the rate of decline has accelerated especially among the young, and further complained that educators and publishers contribute to a 'general culture which does not encourage or reinforce reading.'

An NEA report made national headlines when it revealed that literary reading in America is not only declining rapidly among all groups but the rate of decline has accelerated especially among the young.

- A much-publicized Ithaka Report, *University Publishing in a Digital Age*, reviews the 'seeming[ly] limitless range of opportunities for a faculty member to distribute his or her work, from setting up a web page or blog, to posting an article to a working paper website or institutional repository, to including it in a peer-reviewed journal or book . . . . consequently nearly all intellectual effort results in some form of "publishing."'

What to do? Telling us that reading books is good for us is not persuasive. No one enjoys their leisure behaviour's being judged. That's a losing battle. If it proves true that we prefer getting our news and our entertainment from streaming media, television, and hyperlinked texts, what does that mean for us as human beings? Does the book still matter in our evolution as a species? Will it lose out to content that is born digital?

It's not just information: entire generations of people are said to be 'born digital' as well. What does it mean to call a group the 'digital generation'? First, it presumes access to computers and the Web, and all that this implies. Second, it's simply not true that the current college generation does not read books; they read books when that assignment works for them. The National Association of College Stores has reported that only 30 per cent of their stores are equipped to deliver textbooks as e-books. And at those stores, only 15 per cent of students prefer e-books to printed textbooks.

Our zeal for new technology needs to be tempered with a sceptical awareness of its implications.

A Universal Internet Library

If the United States is a nation built on ideas rather than manufacturing, publishing is the industry where the two meet. Technology is where the expression of desire meets the undertow of fear. Knowledge requires tools that can make our lives smarter, easier, better, and more pleasurable. That is all certainly to the good. But our zeal for new technology needs to be tempered with a sceptical awareness of its implications. As a culture, we are usually better at gauging what there is to gain than at seeing what there is to lose.

Google, of course, is the elephant in the room, the big engine of change. Having scanned the giant libraries of Harvard, Stanford, Michigan, and Oxford and the New York Public Library, Google has made available millions of works that were orphaned by their out-of-print and out-of-copyright status. The stated goal of the Google Books Library Project 'is to work with publishers and libraries to create a comprehensive, searchable, virtual card catalog of all books in all languages that helps users discover new books and publishers discover new readers,' a virtual Alexandria [the site in Egypt of the largest library in the ancient world]. Publishers, while wary, have profited from the disinterment of their deep backlist into the light of day by Google searches. 'The long tail,' made famous by Chris Anderson, shows that only about 2 per cent of the nearly 200,000 books published each year sell more than 5000 copies. The rest are born directly into the long tail, or the remainder bin, the publishing industry's equivalent of 'direct to DVD.'

Writing about the idea of the universal library excites some people to a state of Utopian hysteria. Kevin Kelly is the self-appointed 'Senior Maverick' of *Wired* magazine—you've got to love that title. 'Senior' implies authority; 'maverick' implies iconoclast; together, they grant him the power to call anyone he disagrees with a useless and obstructive dinosaur. (And didn't the last presidential election prove that, given a choice, we don't always prefer a senior maverick?) At any rate, Kelly writes that plans like Google's will allow

> all the books in the world [to] become a single liquid fabric of interconnected words and ideas ... The universal library and its 'books' will be unlike any library or books we have known. Pushing us rapidly toward that Eden of everything, and away from the paradigm of the physical paper tome, is the hot technology of the search-engine.

What these great digital libraries will accomplish, it is hoped, is a conversation among themselves, sharing patterns of use and user-created metadata, recording the behaviours and interests of readers. Books will refer to other books and drill down to source materials, engineered to assist the reader/ user rather than merely record the author. In a sense, these digital libraries will breathe life into the countless numbers of footnotes accumulated over centuries. But even then, they will never be complete. By Google's own estimate, more than 100 million books have been published. Only about 5 or 10 per cent of them are in print. Twenty per cent, printed between the fifteenth century and 1923, are out of copyright; the rest—some 75 per cent of all books ever printed—are 'orphans,' in copyright but out of print. Books are only a part—often a selective synthesis—of the record of human experience. Any claim to an exhaustive and encyclopaedic human record is merely a pipe dream.

Nonetheless, the Google Library project is a great boon to scholars. In 'The Bookless Future,' David A. Bell, a scholar of European history and politics, writes the following fantasy as he is doing research for a book on the culture of war in Napoleonic Europe:

> I am in a coffee shop on my university campus, writing a conference paper. A passage from Edmund Burke's *Letters on a Regicide Peace* comes to mind, but I can't remember the exact wording. Finding the passage, as little as five years ago, would have required going to the library, locating the book on the shelf (or not!), and paging through the text in search of the half-remembered material. Instead, on my laptop, I open Internet Explorer, connect to the wireless campus network. . . . Seconds later, I have found the entire text online. I search for the words 'armed doctrine' and up comes the quote. . . . Total time elapsed: less than one minute.

A pretty cool description (right?) of a brave, new, and hyper-convenient world: scholarship in the humanities and social sciences revolutionized by the new information technology that has put so much primary and secondary source material online. But the great irony, if not blind spot, in this description is that all this hyperlinked research in a world collapsed of time and travel is in service of nothing less than the writing of his next *book*.

To Professor Bell's credit, he quickly darkens his fantasy into dystopian shadows. Will the Internet change 'not only what scholars read but also how they read'? Does reading online tire us more quickly, encourage us to skim, and diminish our actual critical engagement with the text?

The Experience of Reading Online

These are important questions and bear some reflection. First, I'd like to try to get at the experience or character of reading a book online. From the tablet to the scroll to the codex to the printed book, we have been looking for the optimal device for recording information since reading developed. Portability and usability distinguished the book from its inception, which explains why it has lasted some 700 years. Technology did not destroy the concept of the book; it enhanced its nature and quickened its production.

Reading onscreen makes you want to do what is easy to do there: search and discover, strategize how to get at the information you need.

The rise of computers did not, at first, threaten the book. The screens of PCs were friendlier to spreadsheets and information that needed to be scrolled through rather than read through. Users of PCs prefer to toggle between applications rather than proceed sequentially through a linear document. Sustained reading on a large screen makes the eyes glaze over and the back ache. Most troublingly, the concentration fails. Attention wanders. It wants to scan and skim, toggle and hyperlink. Reading onscreen makes you want to do what is easy to do there: search and discover, strategize how to get at the information you need. You are not forced to surrender to the organizing principles established by the author, or to painstakingly follow the path of argumentation she has laid down for you. You won't necessarily have to make marginal notes of themes to trace through the text or circle footnotes whose sources you want to check. Online, it's all a click away.

But you are also missing something important. Searching around in an electronic text, you can skim, cut, and paste, but you will read things out of a deliberate context and sequence. You will get to the 'nut' more quickly, but you will miss learning how the author arrived at her conclusions. Maryanne Wolf, in *Proust and the Squid: The Story and Science of the Reading Brain* writes that 'We are how we read': e-mail, blogs, hyperlinks, pop-up ads, news alerts, and so on require a very different intelligence than that needed for a sustained and deep reading experience. We may become 'mere decoders of information.'

Searching around in an electronic text, you can skim, cut, and paste, but you will read things out of a deliberate context and sequence. You will get to the "nut" more quickly, but you will miss learning how the author arrived at her conclusions.

Open-Ended, Free Form Books

Whether the book can be enhanced by becoming a hypertext online is a very important question for publishers and editors. We need to anticipate the new skills required for preparing texts that will spawn real-time discussions online. Writers will negotiate collaborative development of content that is never static, always expanding. Readers will personalize their books with annotations and hyperlinks to personal journals. The beginning and ending of texts will be porous and shifting; they will lead the reader to discussion forums, social bookmarking sites, and reader reviews and then further open those venues to e-mail lists and social networks. To my mind, all these benefits enhance the experience of deep reading in a book; to some extent, this is what should happen *after* a group of people read a book—whether in a book group or in a classroom that spills over into a café or online.

Is there a downside to this exciting prospect? Only insofar as the futuristic fantasy rejects the centrality of the book. Or sees the book outside the universal library as a fish out of its aquarium, gasping for air. The Institute for the Future of the Book talks about the emergence of the 'networked book': 'the book as a place, as social software . . . , a sustained intellectual experience, a mover of ideas reinvented in a peer to peer ecology. . . . A good future of the book is one that combines the best qualities of physical books with the best qualities of the network.' There will be certain kinds of writers who will want to conduct their research and development in a public way, online, engaged in an open, interdependent model whereby peer review and feedback are reflected in the finished book.

At last, a reasonable, nuanced vision of the future of the book that protects an intellectual legacy and physical craftsmanship while ushering it into a partnership with new technology. Books still matter, in this universe, and will not be replaced by the blogosphere. Even Kevin Kelly admits that 'most of the world's expertise still resides in books.' And, as Alberto Manguel writes, 'It is interesting to note how often a technological development—such as Gutenberg's—promotes rather than eliminates that which it is supposed to supersede.'

Drawbacks of the Digital Text World

One has to wonder whether there will be a cognitive cost to the migration of scholarship away from books. I think of my own behaviour online versus browsing the stacks of a library. When I first came to Yale six years ago, I spent a Saturday wandering the stacks of Sterling Library and wanted nothing more than never to leave the building and to order take-out for the rest of my life. Leave me here; I'll be just fine. Browsing the stacks was an invitation to serendipity; I was excited by the distractions I would find on the way to what I was looking for. Researching online, I feel more as if I were playing a video game, dodging pop-up ads as if fighting asteroids with a joystick. The kinds of things that come my way are impositions rather than accidents, thrown at me by mysterious and possibly venal algorithms rather than discovered by curiosity.

Another discomfiting aspect of the search imperative is that the very agency that allows you to collect information is collecting information about you. Not to sound the Big Brother alarm, it is important to note that, to date, our content providers and search engines are for-profit corporations whose motives are, at best, not transparent. To use the 'collaborative filtering' of some search engines is to dance with a partner who has 'long hands,' as my mother used to warn my sister. Online marketing strategies want to disguise themselves as a service, customized to your needs, rather than a tool to manipulate your desires in a medium too new to learn defences against.

The democratic ideal guarantees that every voice can be heard. But it does not insist that every voice must be heard. Who decides which voice should rise above the noise of the blogosphere, the noise of democracy?

A public annotation of a digital text is called a 'tag,' and I often feel as though I'm playing tag when reading or responding on a blog, strategizing how to outrun, hide from, or make contact with whoever is 'it.' Unlike that singular attention on which the printed book relies, the Internet needs a multiplicity of users who believe in it, like an audience clapping for Tinkerbell to survive. Even as Web indexing proves our online writing to be less original than we thought, we shout louder to be recognized within the din. The question becomes not so much who can be heard as just who ought to be listened to.

The democratic ideal guarantees that every voice can be heard. But it does not insist that every voice *must* be heard. Who decides which voice should rise above the noise of the blogosphere, the noise of democracy?

Defining Books in the Digital Age

Traditionally, that has been the job of the publisher: to select, develop, and edit; to equip with bibliographic back matter; to design and manufacture. In the Age of Information in which research and information are not only accessible but ubiquitous, it is imperative that we ask ourselves the big question: What needs to be a book? Now more than ever. It is no secret that university presses have experienced a crisis in the last decade. Constriction of library budgets, continued specialization, and the professionalization of academic disciplines have diminished the readership of scholarly monographs. Production costs have increased; used books cut into backlist sales. Course packs cannibalize the adoption market for textbooks. We rely more and more on outside subsidies from authors and institutions.

The marketplace demands we ask ourselves the question, What needs to be a book? In particular, what needs to be a scholarly monograph? Aside from tenure and career advancement issues, what does a university press have to publish? And what is a monograph, anyway? *Webster's* has an inelegant definition: 'a written account of a single thing.' The chair of our Publications Committee, David Bromwich, once defined it as 'a work of scholarship that will not sell many copies until it does, at which point it becomes a gem of scholarship.' While there was certainly a twinkle in his eye, his distinction has actually become a useful one, and even prompted a spirited conversation at a recent agenda-less Publications Committee meeting.

We started by thinking about what qualities the scholarly monograph and the gem of scholarship might share:

- original primary research

- blindness to fashion; a love of the ignored and the arcane; providing the culture a way of keeping its neglected history 'warm'

- rigorous methodology

- compound argument, capable of advancing a dozen or more layers of argument

- scholarly apparatus that not only amplifies the text but enables the reader to reconstruct and replicate the original research, to test the author's conclusions, or to use the same material to different ends. Where, then, might the two part company? How could a monograph be cut to reveal its lapidary and gemlike qualities?

- The research demonstrates a passionate commitment, an almost athletic joy in uncovering and managing masses of material.

- The structure invents a new model of managing complexity.

- The prose contributes terminology to the lingua franca of the discipline. It challenges yet can be understood by educated nonspecialists. As [Albert] Einstein is supposed to have said, 'Everything should be as simple as possible, but no simpler.'

- The book crosses disciplines with ease; it listens to its own internal echoes.

- While perhaps narrow in scope, the book feels close. You can feel the breath of the intellect on the page.

You all know what I'm talking about. I'm sure of it. You have all been entranced by the seamlessness of a narrative and dazzled by the marshalling of dozens of arguments in service of a grand theory. You have been transformed within the alchemy of literature. You have been moved by a book.

Books want to enter a relationship in which the best qualities in both print and digital content can be amplified and mutually aggrandized.

The Concept of Books

I hope I have made clear that the defence of the book does not require the trashing of digital culture. Books want to enter a relationship in which the best qualities in both print and digital content can be amplified and mutually aggrandized. The e-reader, for instance, knows that technology does not need to destroy the innovation whose shoulders it stands on. What the Sony Reader and the Amazon Kindle try to do is to simulate the book, to replicate the experience of reading a single book while travelling with the portability of an entire bookshelf of content. So far, sales of these items have been encouraging. Preparing for a long flight to China recently, I myself downloaded some fifty books, ranging from the complete works of Shakespeare to a couple of dozen manuscripts Yale will publish in the next year. I thought I would be the picture of minimalist cool, travelling with a discreet black shoulder bag that housed my Kindle, my BlackBerry, and my iPod. Net weight: four pounds. As I was leaving the house, though, I panicked and shoved six books into my bag. Just in case.

But I may be able to retrain myself here, get used to reading an entire book on a device, like watching a film on a cell phone or shuffling an opera recording on my iPod or eating dinner on a paperless plate every night. But, jokes aside, the prospect of a hyperlinked device that will allow a reader to plug into a portable library of books and related content may be the best argument for why books will still matter.

And if book publishers and digital content providers take each other's counsel, the marriage should work. Publishers will commission, select, edit, peer-review, design, and publish (both in print and electronically) new books. The better the books and the more creative the dissemination, the healthier the university press. And the book is a hardy object; it has survived flood and fire, the Spanish Inquisition, even the US Postal Service. Even if the Internet wanted to kill it, it's got its work cut out.

The book is a hardy object; it has survived flood and fire, the Spanish Inquisition, even the US Postal Service. Even if the Internet wanted to kill it, it's got its work cut out.

A word on the business model. It is not a law of nature that the book, a product of human intelligence and creativity, belongs in the public commons. To argue that books should be given away free is to deny a scholar or writer the right to engage in an act of gainful employment. In order to be morally consistent, those who protest in the public commons that information wants to be free should also advocate that tuitions want to be waived and that professors want to teach without salaries.

That pill is a hard one for the infotopians to swallow. They relish a future in which the universal library is up and running—free of cost and free of books. The question I have for them is, Then what? A bookless world in which people learn to read and research by virtue of snippets and tags and annotations and wiki-research will be a world of people who not only won't be able to read books but won't be able to write them. And the record of human experience, several thousand years evolved, will be irrevocably changed.

One Mind Reaching Another

To my mind, there are two dominant fantasies of reading, each of which is valid, and which cannot help but embody religious tropes, because of the natural affinities that literature and faith have: a deliberate interiority, prolonged concentration, a daily engagement with seriousness of purpose, the working out of a philosophy of how to live one's life.

The first is to look at the Internet as a great big religious metaphor of the cosmic consciousness, the planet's 6 billion minds connected together into the Edenic dream of the universal library. [Cultural critic and philosopher] Walter Benjamin in a letter to [sociologist and philosopher Theodor] Adorno, well before either of them could even conceive of a computer, much less an e-book, wrote: 'The great work of the future will consist of fragments torn from the body of other work; it is a reassembly, a patchwork quilt of meanings already accomplished.'

The second is the image of the individual reader before the universal library. Personally, I collect more books than I need or can possibly read in my lifetime. Visitors to my home sometimes ask, 'Have you really read all of these?' and the answer, of course, is no. That isn't the point. The collector always wants to own more than he can experience all at once. It needs to be enough to overwhelm. Possibility must always overtake satisfaction. A collection is one of the only ways to have too much and not enough at the same time, to be consoled by what cannot be known completely. This is another way in which reading books serve some as a kind of religion.

While immersed in a book, I always feel that that book was meant to be read one reader at a time, written precisely for his or her particular attention, an object waiting to be lit by a singular imagination. The interaction between reader and writer is as intimate as a penitent in prayer. If it is well done, a book will allow you to suspend your awareness of the medium; it wants to be fed to the fires of your attention, to atomize and dematerialize like the Gnostic soul. The other fantasy of reading is the melding of multiple consciousnesses into one giant text, exploding into levels of apprehension enabled by radical technologies. Either apprehension is lit from within by a single and deliberate mind at work to reach another mind.

This is why the book still matters.

12

Books Have Always Survived Predictions of Their Demise

Ben Ehrenreich

Ben Ehrenreich is a journalist and author of The Suitors *and* Ether. *His essays have appeared in the* Nation, *the* Los Angeles Times, *and the* New York Times Magazine. *He is also a visiting professor at the University of California at Riverside.*

The advent of digital publishing has resurrected the arguments of critics who prophesy the demise of printed books. In truth, though, these predictions have been around as long as book culture has existed. What some of these critics forget is that book culture has become part of modern life, regulating it through segmentation of experience and dictating how humans access knowledge and perceive the thoughts of others. Books are not sacred, but they do seem to offer truths waiting to be deciphered by readers. Each work is part of an ongoing narrative of humanity, and thus predictions of the death of the book always appear shortsighted.

Pity the book. It's dead again. Last I checked, Googling "death of the book" produced 11.8 million matches. The day before it was 11.6 milion. It's getting unseemly. Books were once such handsome things. Suddenly they seem clunky, heavy, almost fleshy in their gross materiality. Their pages grow brittle. Their ink fades. Their spines collapse. They are so pitiful, they might as well be human.

The emphasis shifts with each telling, but every writer, editor, publisher, bookseller, and half-attentive reader knows the fundamental story. After centuries of steady climbing, book sales leveled off towards the end of the 1900s. Basic literacy began to plummet. As if television and Reaganomics were not danger enough, some egghead lunatics went and built a web—a web!—out of nothing but electrons. It proved a sneaky and seductive monster. Straight to our offices and living rooms, the web delivered chicken recipes, weather forecasts, pornography, the cutest kitten videos the world had ever seen. But while we were distracted by these glittering gifts, the internet conspired to snare our friend the book, to smother it.

People have been diagnosing—and celebrating—the book's imminent demise for generations.

Early Obituaries for the Book

The alarm at first built gradually. In 1999, Robert Darnton, writing in *The New York Review of Books*, consoled his readers that, all the grim prophecies notwithstanding, "the electronic age did not drive the printed word into extinction." The book seemed safe enough for a few years, in more danger from the avarice of the carbon-based conglomerates that ate up all the publishers, than from anything in silicon. Safe until the fall of 2007, when lady Amazon released her hounds. Within a month of the Kindle's debut, the *New Yorker* was writing of the "Twilight of the Books." (Cue soundtrack: all minor keys, moody cello.) The London *Times* worried that "the slow death of the book may be with us."

Last summer [2010] Amazon announced that it was selling more e-books than the paper kind. The time to fret had passed. It was Kindle vs. kindling. MIT Media Lab co-founder Nicholas Negroponte—whose name is frequently preceded by the word "futurist"—declared that the demise of the paper book should be written in the present tense. "It's happening," Negroponte said, and gave the pulpy artifacts just five years to utterly expire.

None of this is new of course. Nor is it new to point out that people have been diagnosing—and celebrating—the book's imminent demise for generations. It is possible to regard much of Western avant garde poetry and prose as an extended argument with the bound pages from which literature would prefer to break free. In a 1913 manifesto, Filippo Marinetti (a futurist of the OG sort) called for "a typographic revolution directed against the idiotic and nauseating concepts of the outdated and conventional book." His insurrectionary program may now seem quaint—"on the same page we will use three or four colors of ink, or even twenty typefaces if necessary"—but Marinetti was not alone in rebelling against the uniformity imposed on language by the standard typeset page. Similar urges ran through most of the high modernists, certainly through [Gertrude] Stein, [James] Joyce, and [Ezra] Pound, and through the iconoclastic American poet and journalist Robert Carlton Brown (better known as Bob), who, in the late 1920s, envisioned a reading machine designed to liberate words from the static confines of the page. Brown imagined something like a desk-sized microfiche reader capable of displaying spooled celluloid texts called "readies." "Writing has been bottled up in books since the start," he wrote. "It is time to pull out the stopper."

The Book's Regimentation of Modern Life

Not everyone was enthused. F. Scott Fitzgerald bemoaned the deadly consequences of the development of sound cinema—not so much on literature as on his earning capacity as an author. "There was a rankling indignity," he wrote in 1936, "in seeing the power of the written word subordinated to another power, a more glittering, grosser power." But talkies did not kill the book, just as still photography and radio had not and television would not. Far from it: the mass consumption in the US of what we might call serious literature—by which I don't mean the somber stuff so much as the challenging and formally inventive—probably peaked in the late 1960s or early '70s.

The mass consumption in the US of what we might call serious literature—by which I don't mean the somber stuff so much as the challenging and formally inventive—probably peaked in the late 1960s or early '70s.

Most talk of the death of the book in that era was enthusiastically in favor. In 1962, Marshall McLuhan had published an almost spookily prescient book titled *The Gutenberg Galaxy*. It was, among other things, an extended critique of the culture of print. Technology shapes our consciousness, McLuhan argued, and the development of the printed book in the mid-fifteenth century had inaugurated a reorientation of human experience towards the visual, the regimented, the uniform and instrumental. Language, which had once been a wild, uncontainable affair between the oral and aural (think whisper, shout, and song, the playful market-square dynamism of dialect and argot) was silenced, flattened, squeezed into lines evenly arrayed across the rectilinear space between the margins. Spellings were standardized, vernaculars frozen into national languages policed by strict academies. Print, for McLuhan, was the driver behind all that we now recognize as modern. Through it nationalisms arose, and other horrors: capitalism, individualism, alienation. Time itself was emptied out—reduced, like the words on each page, to a linear sequence of homogeneous moments. Print had stolen something. Books had shrunk us. They had "denuded" conscious life. "All experience is segmented and must be processed sequentially," McLuhan mourned. "Rich experience eludes the wretched mesh or sieve of our attention."

An end was in sight. We had already entered a "new electric age" characterized by interdependence rather than segmentation. "The world has become a computer," McLuhan wrote, "an electronic brain, exactly as in an infantile piece of science fiction." The Internet was still a Cold-War fantasy, but for McLuhan print's corpse was already growing cold. (He dated the collapse of the "Gutenberg Galaxy" to 1905 and Einstein's early work on relativity.) This was not necessarily cause for optimism. McLuhan coined the phrase "global village" to describe the hyper-networked world that was already taking shape. He had no illusions, though, about the nobility of village life. Our newly TV-, telephone-, and radio-enwebbed multiverse could just as easily be ruled by "panic terrors . . . befitting a world of tribal drums" as by any bright pastoral harmony. And so it was and is.

The book for [Jacques] Derrida stood in for an entire metaphysics that reached back through all of Western thought: a conception of existence as a text that could be deciphered.

In 1967, when Jacques Derrida took up the theme of "the end of the book" in *Of Grammatology*, McLuhan's ideas were still sufficiently in the air that the philosopher could refer to "this death of the civilization of the book of which so much is said" without need for further explanation. But the "civilization of the book," for Derrida, meant more than the era of moveable type. It preceded Gutenberg, and even the medieval rationalists who wrote of "the book of nature" and via that metaphor understood the material world as revelation analogous to scripture. The book for Derrida stood in for an entire metaphysics that reached back through all of Western thought: a conception of existence as a text that could be deciphered, a text with a stable meaning lodged somewhere outside of language. "The idea of the book is the idea of a totality," he wrote. "It is the encyclopedic protection of theology and of logocentrism against the disruption of writing, against its aphoristic energy and . . . against difference in general." Those, in case you couldn't tell, are fighting words.

Nostalgia for the Book Object

It is perhaps a symptom of print's decline that the current conversation about the book's demise has forgotten all these other ones. Instead we shuttle between two equally hollow poles: goofball digital boosterism a la Negroponte on one side and on the other a helpless, anguished nostalgia for the good old days of papercuts. Call it biblionecrophilia: the retreat of the print-faithful into a sort of autistic fetishization of the book-as-object—as if [Amazon.com founder and CEO] Jeff Bezos could be convinced to lay e-profits aside by recalling for a moment the soft, woody aroma of a yellow-paged Grove Press paperback; as if there were nothing more to books than paper, ink, and glue.

For the record, my own loyalties are uncomplicated. I adore few humans more than I love books. I make no promises, but I do not expect to purchase a Kindle or a Nook or any of their offspring. I hope to keep bringing home bound paper books until my shelves snap from their weight, until there is no room in my apartment for a bed or a couch or another human being, until the floorboards collapse and my eyes blur to dim. But the book, bless it, is not a simple thing.

The book as an affordable object of mass production—as something directly akin to the books that line our shelves—was not born until the 19th century, just in time for the early announcements of its death.

Nor, as we know it, is it particularly venerable. All of our words for book refer, at root, to forms no longer recognizable as such: *biblos* being the Greek word for the pith of the papyrus stalk (on which texts in the Greco-Roman world were inscribed); *libri* being Latin for the inner bark of a tree, just as the Old English *bóc* and Old Norse *bók* referred to the beech tree. Likewise "tome" is from a Greek word for a cutting (of papyrus) and "volume" is from the Latin for a rolled-up thing—a scroll, which is the form most texts took until they were replaced by folded parchment codices. Prior to the late 13th century, when paper was first brought to Europe from China, the great works of Western civilization were recorded on the skins of animals. The Inca wrote by knotting strings. The ancient Chinese scrawled calligraphy on cliffs. (Do mountains count as books?) The printed, paper book, as we know it, dates only to the mid-fifteenth century, but those early Gutenberg exemplars were hardly something you'd curl up with on a rainy Sunday afternoon. The book as an affordable object of mass production—as something directly akin to the books that line our shelves—was not born until the 19th century, just in time for the early announcements of its death.

But what could it mean for the book to die? Which sort of book? And what variety of death? What if the book had only ever lived by dying? What if it were only ever present through its absence, like the figure of the book that is sketched over the many volumes of Edmond Jabès' poetry, so loved by Derrida? ("The book dives and drowns in books still to be written which are only its repeated efforts to escape death or, rather, the illegibility to which it is pledged.") Or like the uppercase Book described by Bruno Schulz, who opened his 1937 collection *Sanatorium under the Sign of the Hourglass* with an odd and wonder-filled short story titled simply, "The Book." Four years after its publication, German troops marched into the small southeastern Polish city of Drogobych, where Schulz lived. And though Schulz was Jewish (as was Jabès, not at all coincidentally), he resisted his friends' attempts to smuggle him to safety. Two years into the occupation, Schulz was shot in the street by the SS, his own last book—*The Messiah*, he called it—unfinished and now lost for good.

In the world of Schulz's fiction, The Book is, to borrow a tic from Derrida, always already lost. The story opens with a coy admission of defeat: "I am simply calling it The Book without any epithets or qualifications," Schulz begins, confessing "a shade of helplessness . . . for no word, no allusion, can adequately suggest the shiver of fear, the presentiment of a thing without name that exceeds all our capacity for wonder." Of course words are all he has, and with them he goes on to recall the Book from a hazy, near-forgotten epoch "somewhere in the dawn of childhood," when he saw it lying on his father's desk. Sometimes, when his father was away, the child narrator would watch as birds—whole "flocks of swallows and larks"— erupted from its pages. Sometimes the wind opened it "like a huge cabbage rose [and] the petals, one by one, eyelid under eyelid, all blind, velvety, and dreamy, slowly disclosed a blue pupil, a colored peacock's heart, or a chattering nest of hummingbirds."

Then, for years perhaps—chronology is more than hazy here—the Book disappears from memory. One night it returns to the narrator in a dream. He wakes and scours the shelves. He demands that his parents tell him what's become of it. They humor him, pushing various volumes into his hands. His father hands him a Bible and he scoffs: "Why do you give me that . . . clumsy falsification? What have you done with The Book?"

Here Schulz parts ways with all but the most heretical of his own People of the Book. The text Schulz's narrator is searching for exceeds the virtue of any mere Torah scroll. It's nothing as banal as the old Book of Nature either. The father tries to deny that it exists, to belittle it as a childish fiction we all grow out of—like Santa Claus or a god that loves us. The narrator knows better: "I knew then that The Book is a postulate, that it is a goal." Soon after, when the housekeeper laughs aloud at an ad for a miraculous hair tonic ("I, Anna Csillag, born at Karlovice in Moravia, had a poor growth of hair . . ."), the narrator grabs a sheaf of "advertisements and personal announcements" from her hands, recognizing in it, "The Book, its last pages, the unofficial supplement, the tradesman's entrance full of refuse and trash!" She had been tearing out its pages all along to wrap his father's lunches.

The Unfinished Word

Like all of Schulz's fictions, "The Book" is set in an atmosphere of painful, almost unfathomable drabness—think wintry provincial Poland, all the world "a gray and empty Tuesday"—but one over which reality is stretched like a delicate skin, a membrane shivering with infinite possibility. So it is here: in print's crudest manifestation, in a mail-order catalog, he finds vestiges of "the authentic Book, the holy original." Its pages hawk miracle cures, barrel organs, songbirds, the services of "a certain Mme. Magda Wang," experienced in "the 'dressage' of men."

Soon, all these advertised offerings have climbed from their columns of print, rebelling against the dull tyranny of margins. They take over the story. Legions of cripples, relieved of their ailments by one magic elixir and graced by another with prodigious growths of hair, cast aside their crutches and march off through the "white villages steeped in prose and drabness." They follow their leader, Anna Csillag, like an "odyssey of beavers, roaming from town to town with barrel organs," singing aloud as bright multitudes of finches take flight from their instruments. The Book is not all joy and birdsong, though even its darkness titillates: the village the cripples leave behind will be shortly taken over by "the cynical and perverse Magda Wang."

Towards the end of the story, Schulz reveals "a strange characteristic of the script, which by now no doubt has become clear to the reader: it unfolds while being read, its boundaries open to all currents and flexibilities." And so it turns out that after all that searching, The Book—dead again and lost forever, living only in hoarse echoes and degraded traces—has not been written yet. The world is unfinished and "god" a word half-spoken. The Book is a mountain, a goat-skin, a forest, a slab of clay, a knotted string, a blinking screen, a reed, a flock of finches. It is a chorus line of electrons. Don't freak out. You can't buy it or sell it no matter what you do. You'd be a fool to want to own it. Except through writing it and reading it and participating thereby in its creation—The Book always eludes us. Until we're done, which may be soon, books will be with us: dead as always, the picture of health.

Organizations to Contact

The editors have compiled the following list of organizations concerned with the issues debated in this book. The descriptions are derived from materials provided by the organizations. All have publications or information available for interested readers. The list was compiled on the date of publication of the present volume; the information provided here may change. Be aware that many organizations take several weeks or longer to respond to inquiries, so allow as much time as possible.

American Library Association (ALA)
50 E. Huron St., Chicago, IL   60611
(800) 545-2433 • fax: (312) 440-9374
e-mail: ala@ala.org
website: www.ala.org

The American Library Association is an organization with the stated goal of promoting library service and librarianship in the United States. As such, it currently focuses on seven key areas to achieve this purpose: Advocating on behalf of libraries and the profession, promoting diversity, enabling continuing education opportunities for those in the field as well as opportunities for lifelong learning for all, ensuring equal access to information and library services, preserving intellectual freedom, improving literacy rates, and fostering excellence within all library organizations. One of the emerging issues the organization is currently focusing on is e-books and libraries. The ALA website dedicated to this topic explores such issues as copyright, licensing and terms of use, access, and First Amendment concerns. Publications of the ALA include *American Libraries, Booklist,* and *ALA TechSource.*

Association of American Publishers (AAP)
455 Massachusetts Ave. NW, Ste. 700
Washington, DC   20001-2777
(202) 347-3375 • fax: (202) 347-3690
website: www.publishers.org

The Association of American Publishers is a membership organization representing three hundred companies of the publishing industry in the United States. The association advocates on behalf of the industry and produces communications for its members regarding legislative and regulatory issues, both in the United States and around the world. Information about the impact of e-books on the publishing industry can be found on the AAP website.

Authors Guild

31 E. Thirty-Second St., 7th Fl., New York, NY 10016
(212) 563-5904 • fax: (212) 564-5363
e-mail: staff@authorsguild.org
website: www.authorsguild.org

The Authors Guild has served as the primary advocate of copyright protection, fair contracts, and free expression for writers in America for nearly a century. Published writers can become members and receive legal assistance as well as services, such as discounted health insurance, aid in creating an Internet presence, and admittance to guild panels and programs. Information about the impact of technology and e-books on writers and publishers can be found in such articles as "How Apple Saved Barnes & Noble. Probably," "E-book Royalty Math: The House Always Wins," and "The E-book Royalty Mess: An Interim Fix," all available on the Authors Guild website.

Internet Archive (IA)

300 Funston Ave., San Francisco, CA 94118
(415) 561-6767 • fax: (415) 840-0391
e-mail: info@archive.org
website: www.archive.org

The Internet Archive has been working since its founding in 1996 to create a comprehensive Internet library with permanent, open, and free access to digitized historical collections of information to preserve these artifacts for future generations. The organization believes that since the tendency has been from paper to digital in recent years, it is necessary to collect and maintain digital collections to ensure their preservation. While the organization has historically focused on the importance of digitization, it has recently established a Physical Archive of the Internet Archive in an attempt to preserve one copy of every book, record, or movie digitized. More information about the Internet Archive's ongoing projects can be found on the organization's website.

Library of Congress

101 Independence Ave. SE, Washington, DC   20540
(202) 707-5000
website: www.loc.gov

The Library of Congress serves as both a national cultural institution as well as the research arm of Congress with the dual mission of aiding Congress in performing its functions as stated by the Constitution and providing the materials necessary to enhance the knowledge of the American citizenry. Its buildings house millions of books, recordings, photographs, maps, and manuscripts. In keeping with the advancement of technology, the library has begun digitizing its collection with detailed information about this process available online.

National Book Critics Circle (NBCC)

160 Varick St., 11th Fl., New York, NY   10013
e-mail: info@bookcritics.org
website: www.bookcritics.org

The National Book Critics Circle has been working since its founding in 1974 to recognize excellence in literature and encourage ongoing discussion about reading, critique, and writing. It presents awards annually in such literary categories as autobiography, biography, criticism, fiction, nonfiction, and poetry. In light of the ongoing impact of technology on reading, writing, and reviewing, the organization has dedicated much of its attention to examining how changes to the publishing industry and the delivery of written content has impacted cultural connection with written materials. Information about this topic can be found on the NBCC website and on its blog, *Critical Mass.*

Project Gutenberg Literary Archive Foundation
809 N. 1500 West, Salt Lake City, UT   84116
e-mail: help2010@pglaf.org
website: www.gutenberg.org

Project Gutenberg was founded in 1971 by Michael Hart in an attempt to make e-books available online, free of charge. Books currently available on the site include those that are in the public domain—that is, no longer covered under copyright laws—and those whose owners have granted the site permission to publish them online. This site was the first digital library and provides most of its e-books in plain text form, making them accessible to almost all individuals with Internet access. Volunteers power the project and are responsible for much of the content that has been uploaded to the site—over thirty-six thousand works as of June 2011. More information about Project Gutenberg and access to its collection can be found on the project's website.

TechSoup for Libraries
TechSoup Global, 435 Branna St., Ste. 100
San Francisco, CA   94107
(415) 633-9300
e-mail: techsoupforlibraries@techsoup.org
website: www.techsoupforlibraries.org

A project of TechSoup Global, TechSoup for Libraries works to help nonprofits and libraries around the world acquire technology and technology education at an affordable price. Much of the work has focused on helping libraries to incorporate electronic books and e-readers into existing infrastructure. Articles such as "Are E-readers Greener than Books?" and "New E-reader Technologies and Social Benefit Organizations" have explored some of the possibilities of these new technologies.

Bibliography

Books

Matthew Battles — *Library: An Unquiet History.* New York: Norton, 2003.

Mark Bauerlein — *The Dumbest Generation: How the Digital Age Stupefies Young Americans and Jeopardizes Our Future.* New York: Jeremy P. Tarcher/Penguin, 2008.

Sven Birkerts — *The Gutenberg Elegies: The Fate of Reading in an Electronic Age.* New York: Faber and Faber, 1994.

John Brockman — *Is the Internet Changing the Way You Think? The Net's Impact on Our Minds and Future.* New York: HarperCollins, 2011.

Nicholas Carr — *The Shallows: What the Internet Is Doing to Our Brains.* New York: Norton, 2011.

Robert Darnton — *The Case for Books: Past, Present, and Future.* New York: PublicAffairs, 2009.

David Finkelstein and Alistair McCleery — *An Introduction to Book History.* New York: Routledge, 2005.

Jeff Gomez — *Print Is Dead: Books in Our Digital Age.* New York: Macmillan, 2008.

Nicole Howard   *The Book: The Life Story of a Technology*. Westport, CT: Greenwood, 2005.

Maggie Jackson   *Distracted: The Erosion of Attention and the Coming Dark Age*. New York: Prometheus, 2008.

Alan Jacobs   *The Pleasures of Reading in an Age of Distraction*. New York: Oxford University Press, 2011.

Marilyn Johnson   *This Book Is Overdue! How Librarians and Cybrarians Can Save Us All*. New York: HarperCollins, 2010.

Andrew Keen   *The Cult of the Amateur: How Blogs, MySpace, YouTube, and the Rest of Today's User-Generated Media Are Destroying Our Economy, Our Culture, and Our Values*. New York: Doubleday, 2009.

Geoffrey Nunberg   *The Future of the Book*. Berkeley and Los Angeles: University of California Press, 1996.

John Palfrey and   *Born Digital: Understanding the First Urs Gasser   Generation of Digital Natives*. New York: Basic Books, 2008.

Ted Striphas   *The Late Age of Print: Everyday Book Culture from Consumerism to Control*. New York: Columbia University Press, 2009.

David Trend   *The End of Reading: From Gutenberg to Grand Theft Auto*. New York: Peter Lang, 2010.

David L. Ulin — *The Lost Art of Reading: Why Books Matter in a Distracted Time.* Seattle: Sasquatch, 2010.

Periodicals

Spencer E. Ante — "Trying to Avert a Digital Horror Story," *BusinessWeek*, January 11, 2010.

Ken Auletta — "Publish or Perish," *New Yorker*, April 26, 2010.

Anne Behler and Binky Lush — "Are You Ready for E-readers?," *Reference Librarian*, January–June 2011.

Damon Brown — "The Digital Landscape," *Kirkus Reviews*, January 15, 2011.

Robert Darnton — "On the Ropes?," *Publishers Weekly*, September 14, 2009.

William C. Dougherty — "Managing Technology: E-readers: Passing Fad or Trend of the Future?," *Journal of Academic Librarianship*, May 2010.

Ross Duncan — "Ebooks and Beyond: The Challenge for Public Libraries," *APLIS*, June 2010.

William Germano — "What Are Books Good For?," *Chronicle of Higher Education*, October 1, 2010.

Jamie E. Helgren — "Booking to the Future," *American Libraries*, January–February 2011.

Kevin Kelly   "From Print to Pixel," *Smithsonian*,
                         July/August 2010.

Nicole Krauss   "Writer's Block," *New Republic*,
                         March 24, 2011.

Chuck Leddy   "The Changing Future of Books,"
                         Writer, April 2010.

Steven Levy   "The Future of Reading," *Newsweek*,
                         November 26, 2007.

Molly Marsh   "Are Books Obsolete?," *Sojourners*,
                         May 2009.

Patrick   "What Happens at the End of the
McCormick   Book?," *U.S. Catholic*, August 2009.

Rob Nugent   "The Decline of Reading in an Age
                         of Ignorance," *Quadrant Magazine*,
                         January 2011.

John Podhoretz   "The Tolstoy App," *Commentary*,
                         February 2010.

David Pogue   "The Trouble with E-readers,"
                         Scientific American, November 2010.

Ralph Raab   "Books and Literacy in the Digital
                         Age," *American Libraries*, August
                         2010.

Ramin Setoodeh   "The Future of the Book," *Newsweek*,
and Jennie   February 14, 2011.
Yabroff

Margaret Simons   "Reading in an Age of Change,"
                         Overland, Fall 2010.

William Skidelsky   "Death of the Book?," *New Statesman*, September 29, 2008.

David J. Staley   "The Future of the Book in a Digital Age," *Futurist*, September–October 2003.

Roger Sutton   "When A Is for App," *Horn Book Magazine*, November–December 2010.

Emily Williams   "Copyright, E-books and the Unpredictable Future," *Publishing Research Quarterly*, March 2011.

Index

CPSIA information can be obtained
at www.ICGtesting.com
Printed in the USA
FFOW030924151212
558FF